yumisakugawa

FASHION PREDICTIONS
THIS HAIRSTYLE
NO EYEBROWS
FAKE EYEBROWS MADE OF STICK-ON GLITTER
IKEBANA REALNESS BIO-FASHION
TERRARIUM PENDANTS

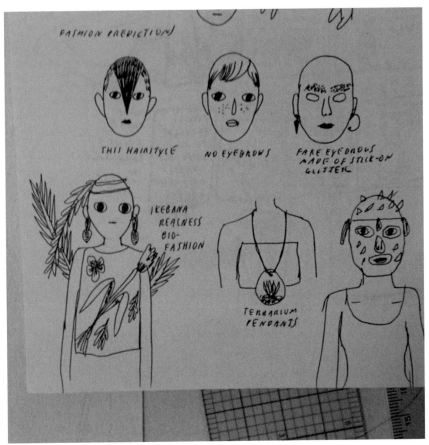

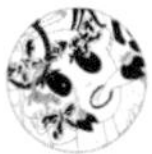

Liked by **tinypyramid**, **saewwwon** and **178 others**

yumisakugawa A while back I was bored and made fashion forecasts

View all 12 comments

JUNE 26, 2014

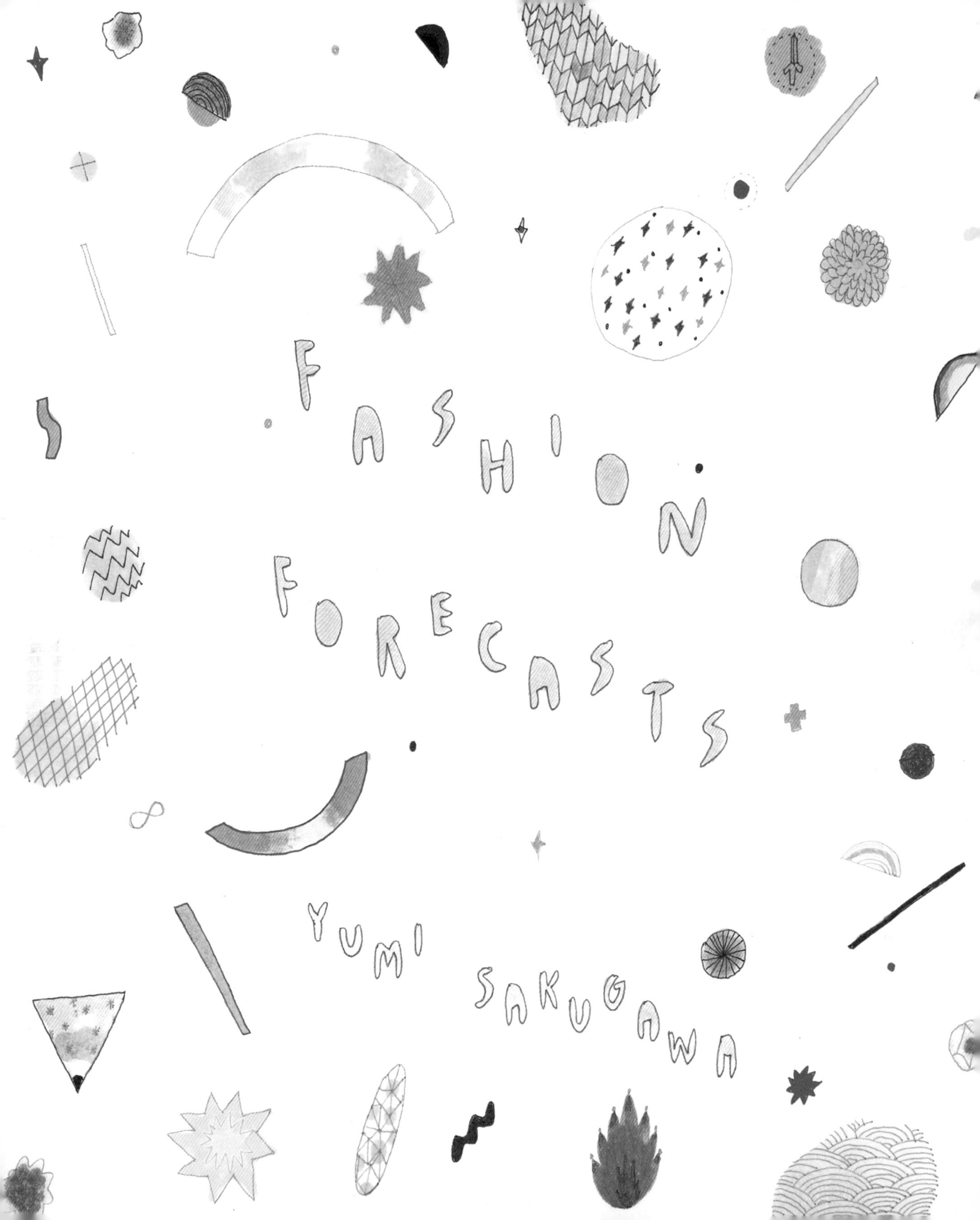
FASHION FORECASTS
YUMI SAKUGAWA

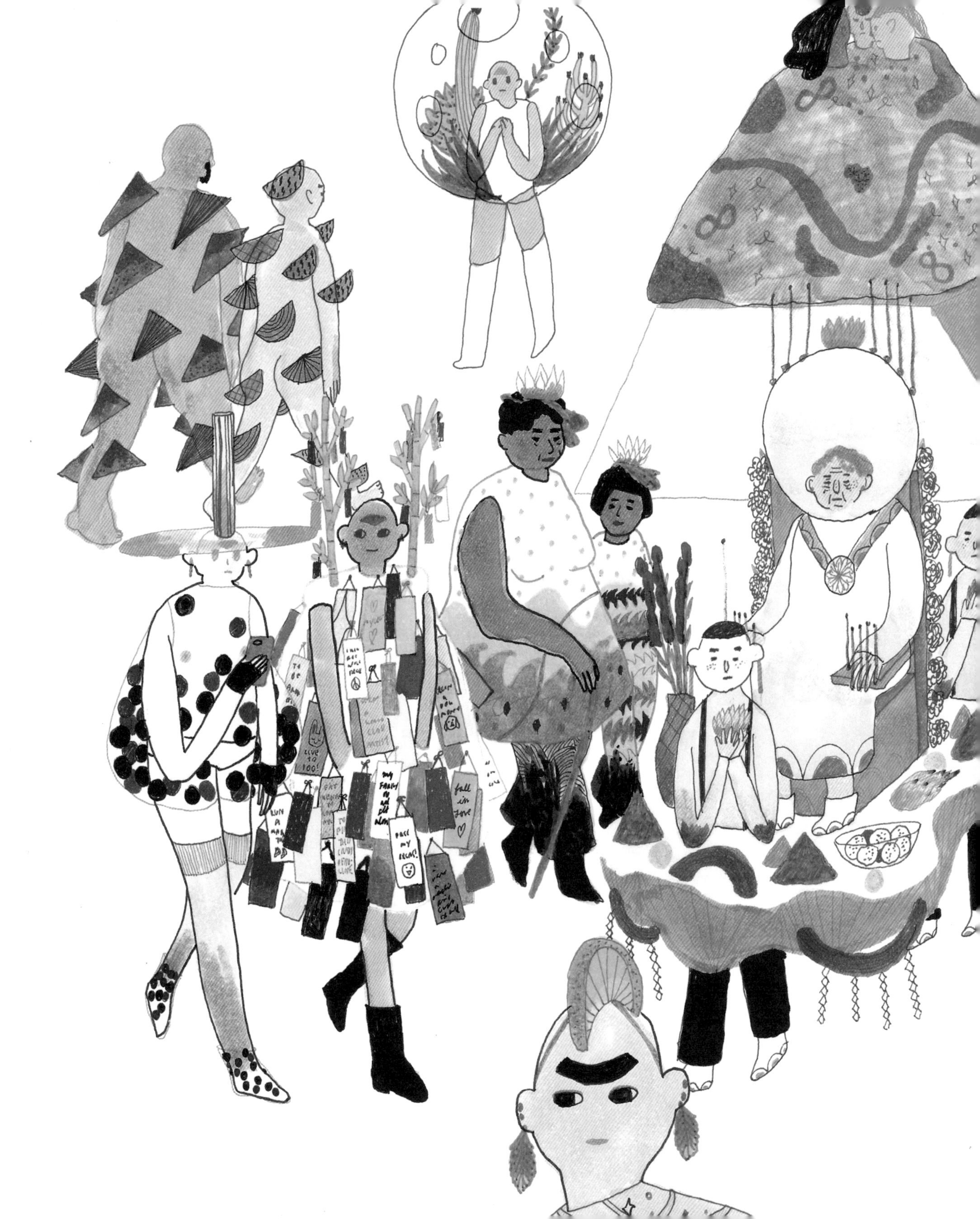

LIVE TO 100!
fall in love
PASS MY EXAMS!

FACE

HAIR

BODY

GEOMETRIC UNIBROW

OMBRÉ UNIBROW
HAIR

ARMPIT HAIR
EXTENSION
INFINITY SCARF

ORANGE KAWAII REALNESS
(ACCENTUATING YOUR LARGE
FACIAL PORES BY DYEING
YOUR FACE ORANGE AND LOOKING
LIKE AN ORANGE.)

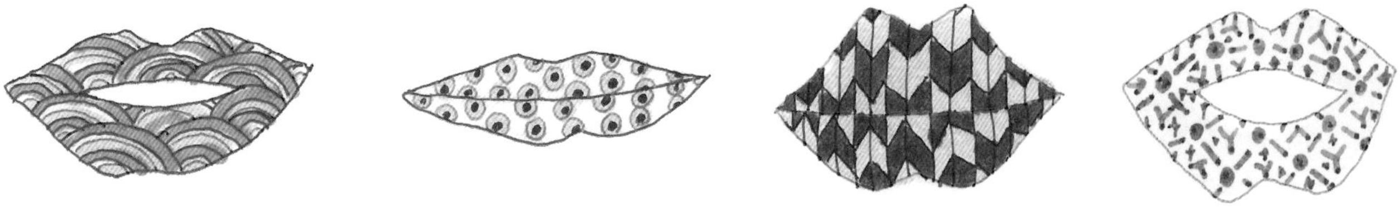

TRADITIONAL TEXTILE LIP DECALS

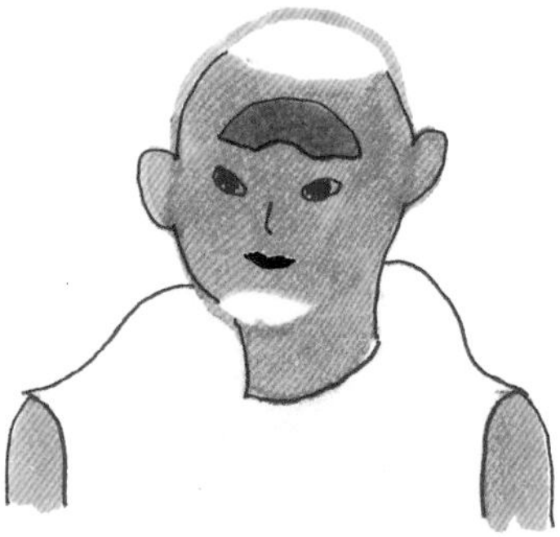

CHIN/SKULL SHADOW

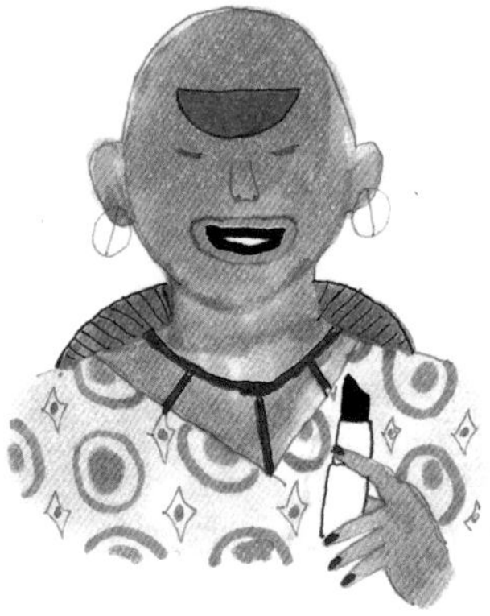

TEETHSTICK

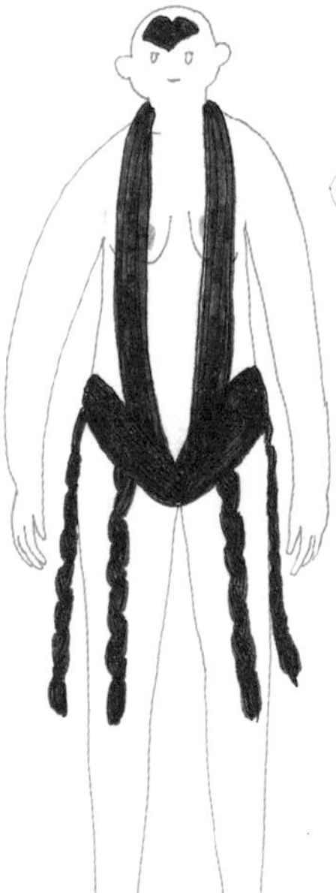

PUBIC HAIR
BODY SUIT

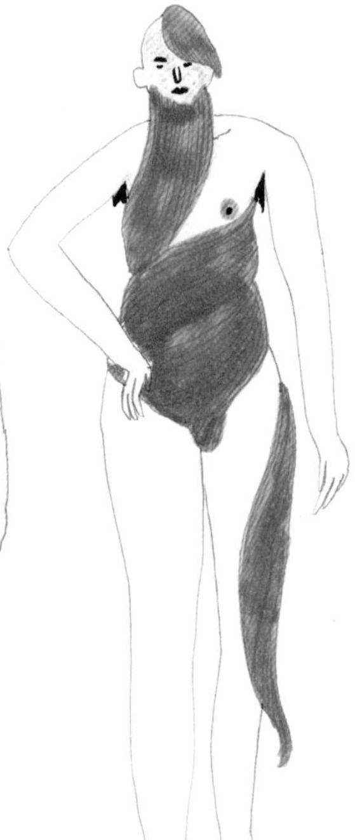

BEARD
WRAP DRESS

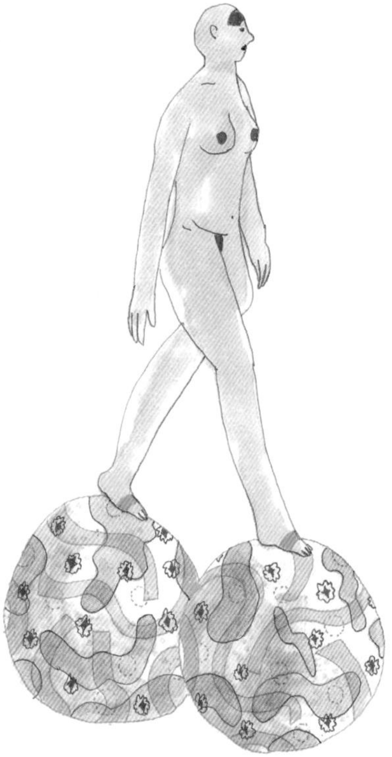

NAKED EXCEPT FOR
BALL HEELS

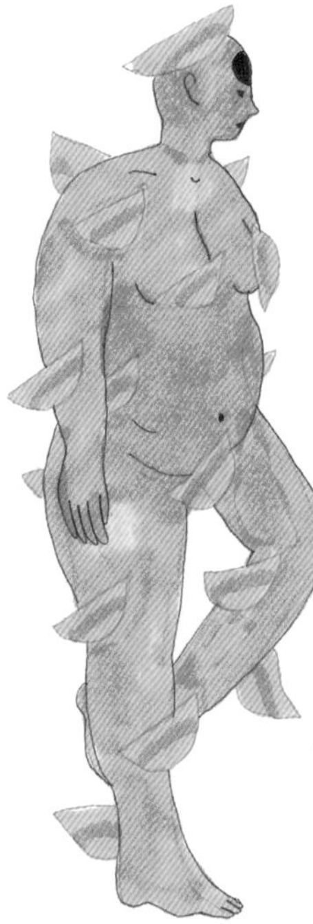

NON-COHESIVE
FABRIC STICK-ONS

MINDFUL MAKE UP RITUAL

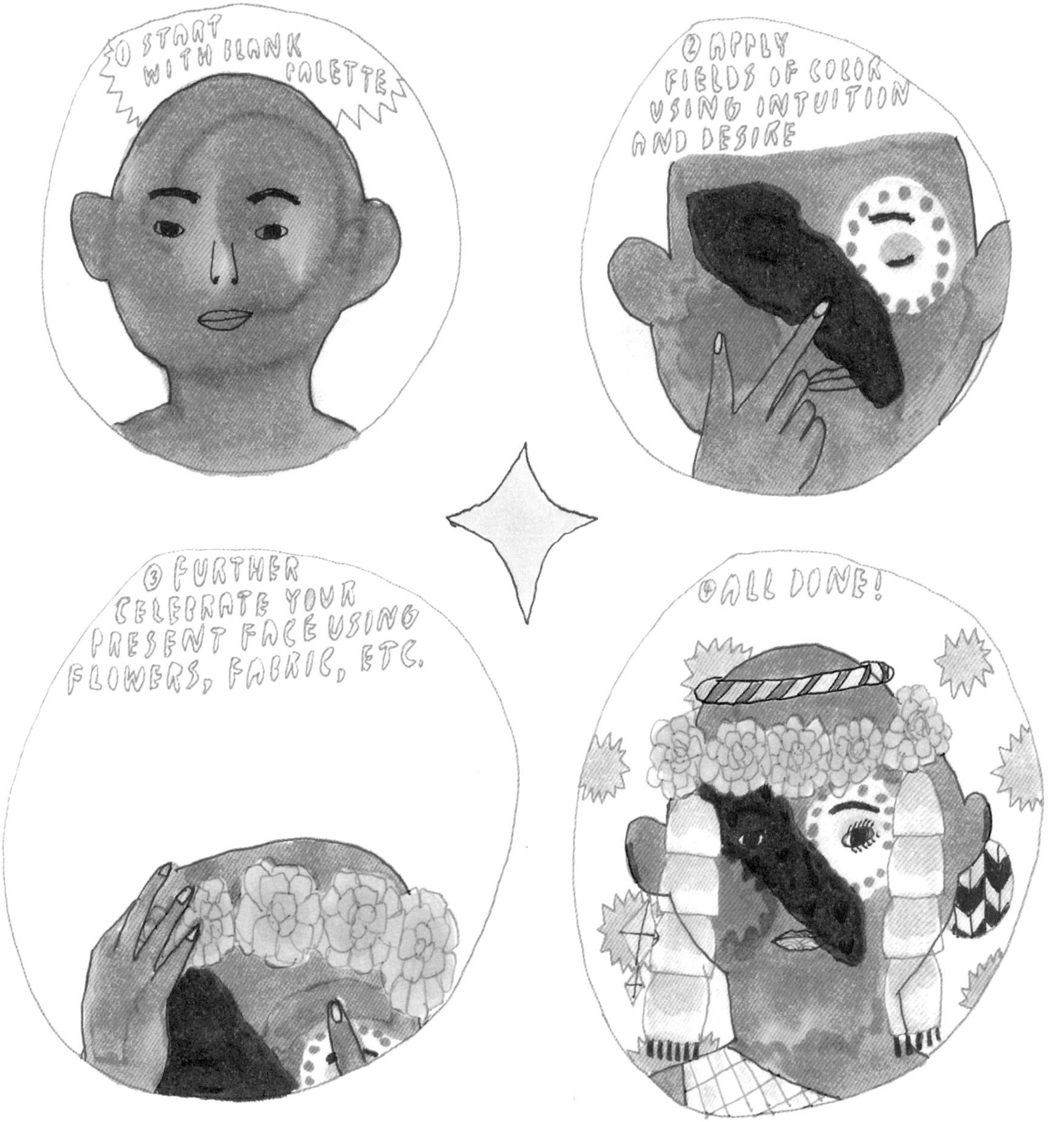
① START WITH BLANK PALETTE
② APPLY FIELDS OF COLOR USING INTUITION AND DESIRE
③ FURTHER CELEBRATE YOUR PRESENT FACE USING FLOWERS, FABRIC, ETC.
④ ALL DONE!

FOOD

INSPIRED

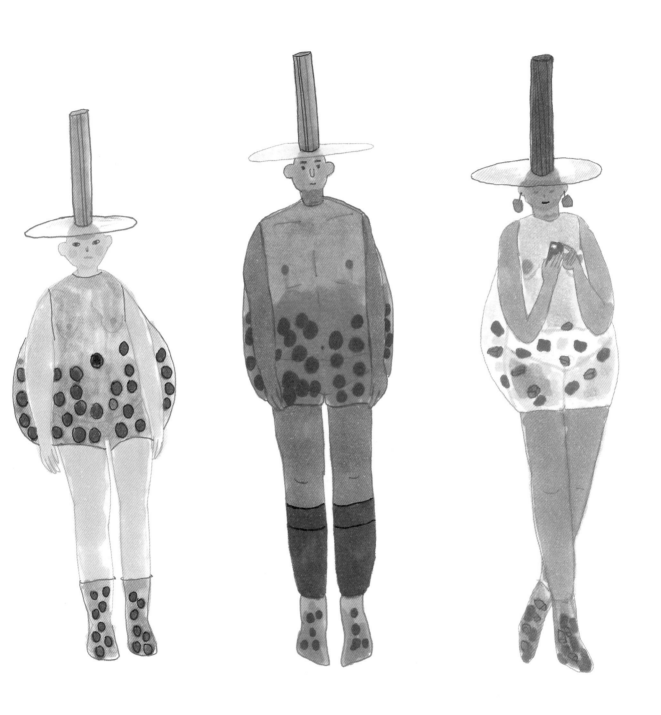

BOBA / BUBBLE TEA DRESS

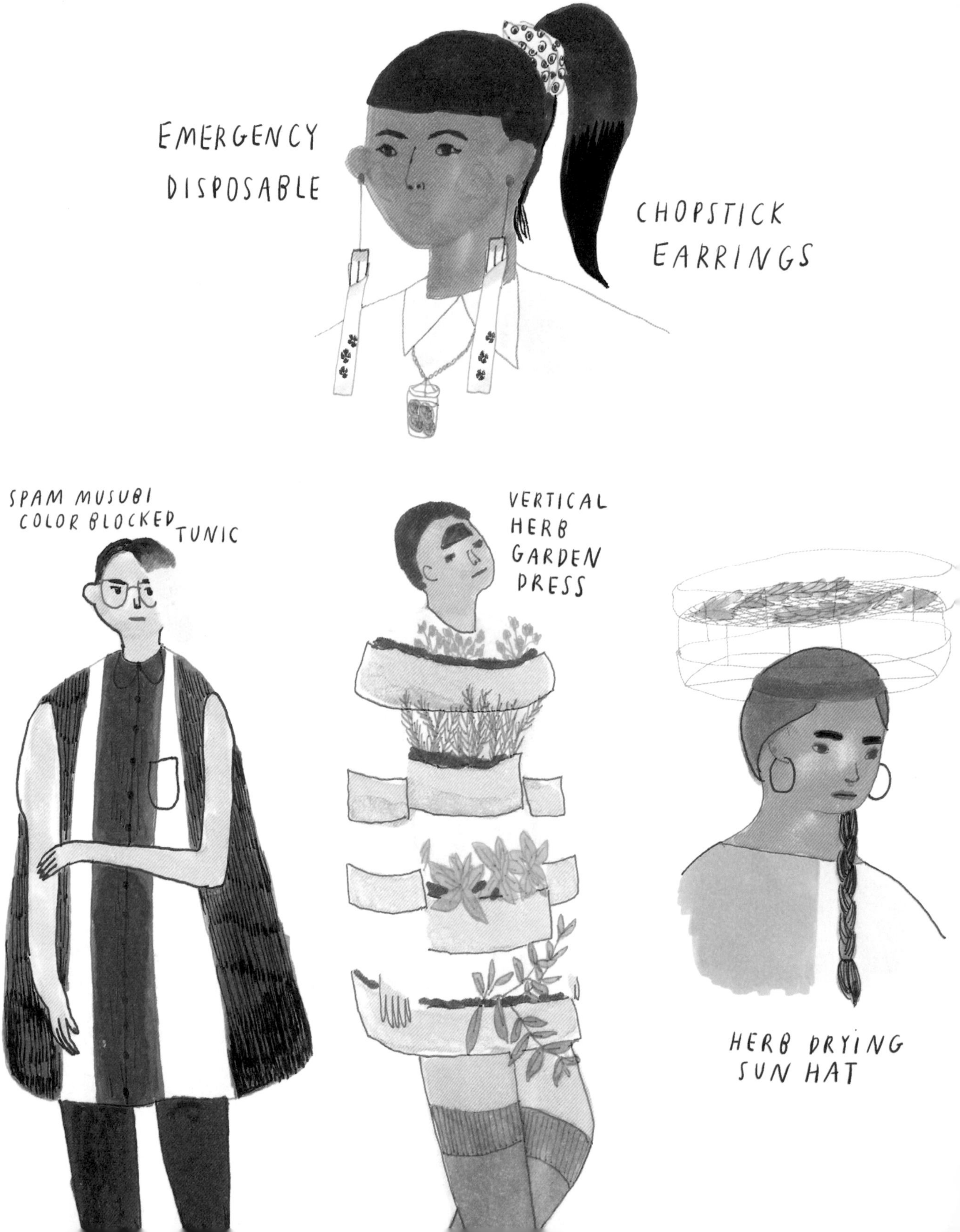
EMERGENCY DISPOSABLE
CHOPSTICK EARRINGS
SPAM MUSUBI COLOR BLOCKED TUNIC
VERTICAL HERB GARDEN DRESS
HERB DRYING SUN HAT

PHO DRESS

PEARLS OF BEADY FAT

CHILI OIL RED BEADS

HALF SUBMERGED RICE NOODLES AND ONIONS

INSPIRED BY LEFTOVER BROTH NESTLING AT THE BOTTOM OF AN ALMOST FINISHED BOWL OF PHO.

KIMCHI JAR DRESS

ABSTRACT PRINT AND COLOR PALETTE INSPIRED BY JAR OF KIMCHI AS SEEN FROM THE OUTSIDE.

FAMILY

ELDERLY

ANCESTRAL

WORSHIP

FASHION BECOMES PERFORMATIVE
AND INTERGENERATIONAL

EMBRACING

BOTH THE

VERY YOUNG

AND

VERY OLD

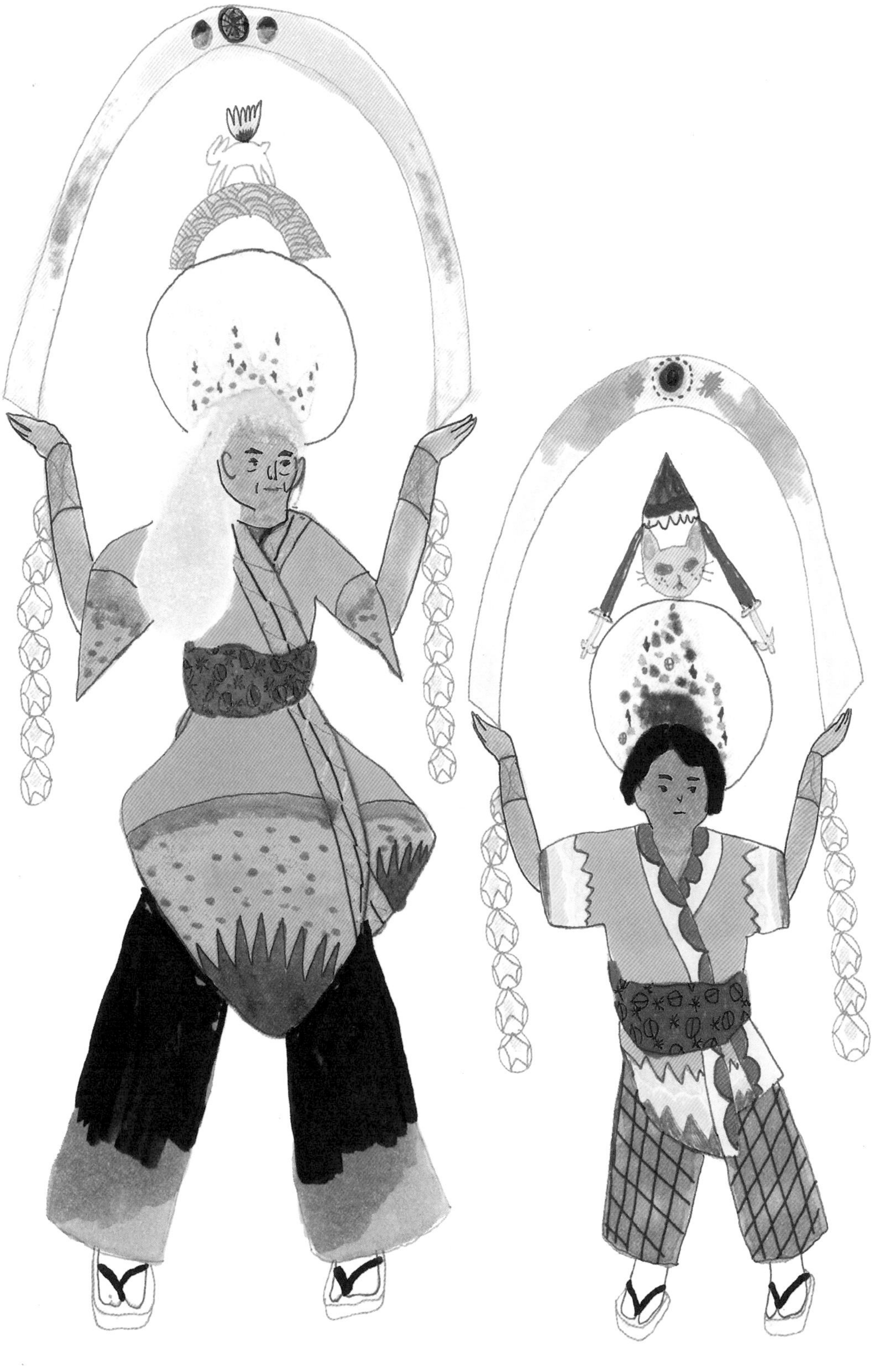

GOLD GLITTER WRINKLES

THE EMERGENCE OF NEW
WRINKLES ARE CELEBRATED
AND MADE MORE OBVIOUS
WITH GOLD GLITTER.

CELEBRATORY BIRTHDAY CAPE

WORN EVERY BIRTHDAY
AGE 60+, A DIFFERENT
COLOR PALETTE/DESIGN
FOR EVERY YEAR.

GOLD THRONE CHAIR BELT

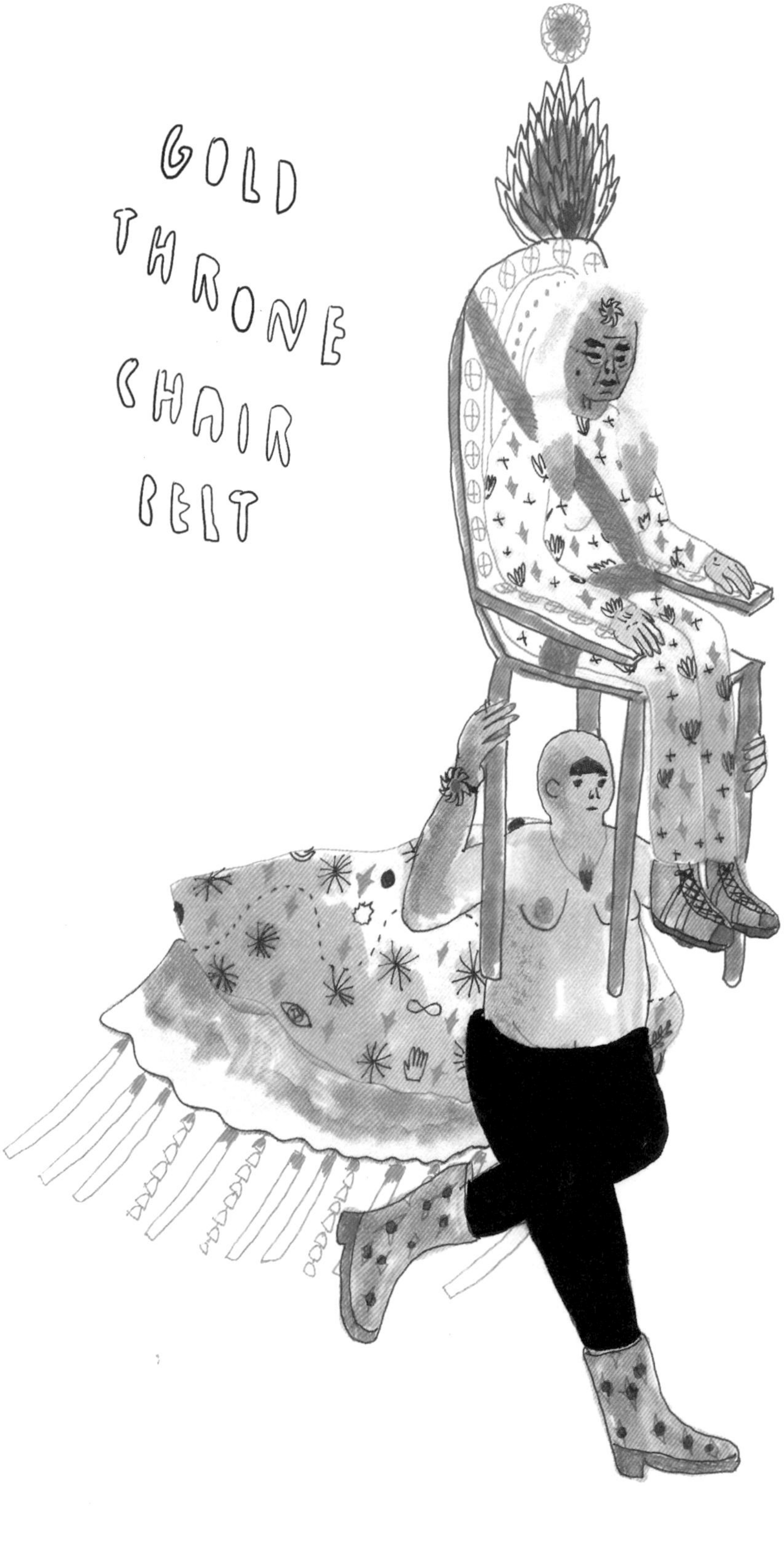

RESPECTFUL, STRONG, AND ABLE-BODIED ATTENDANT NOT INCLUDED.

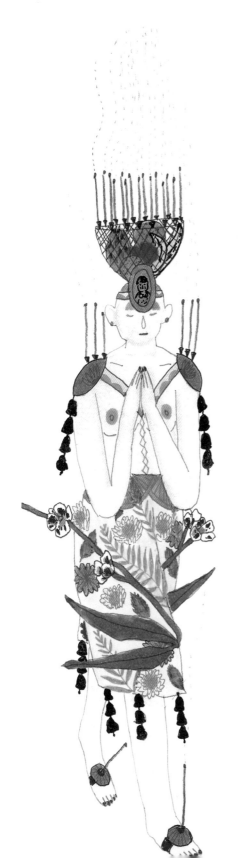

FAMILY
ALTAR
ANCESTRAL
WORSHIP
CEREMONIAL
EVERYDAY
WEAR

PLANT
LIFE

ENVIRONMENT

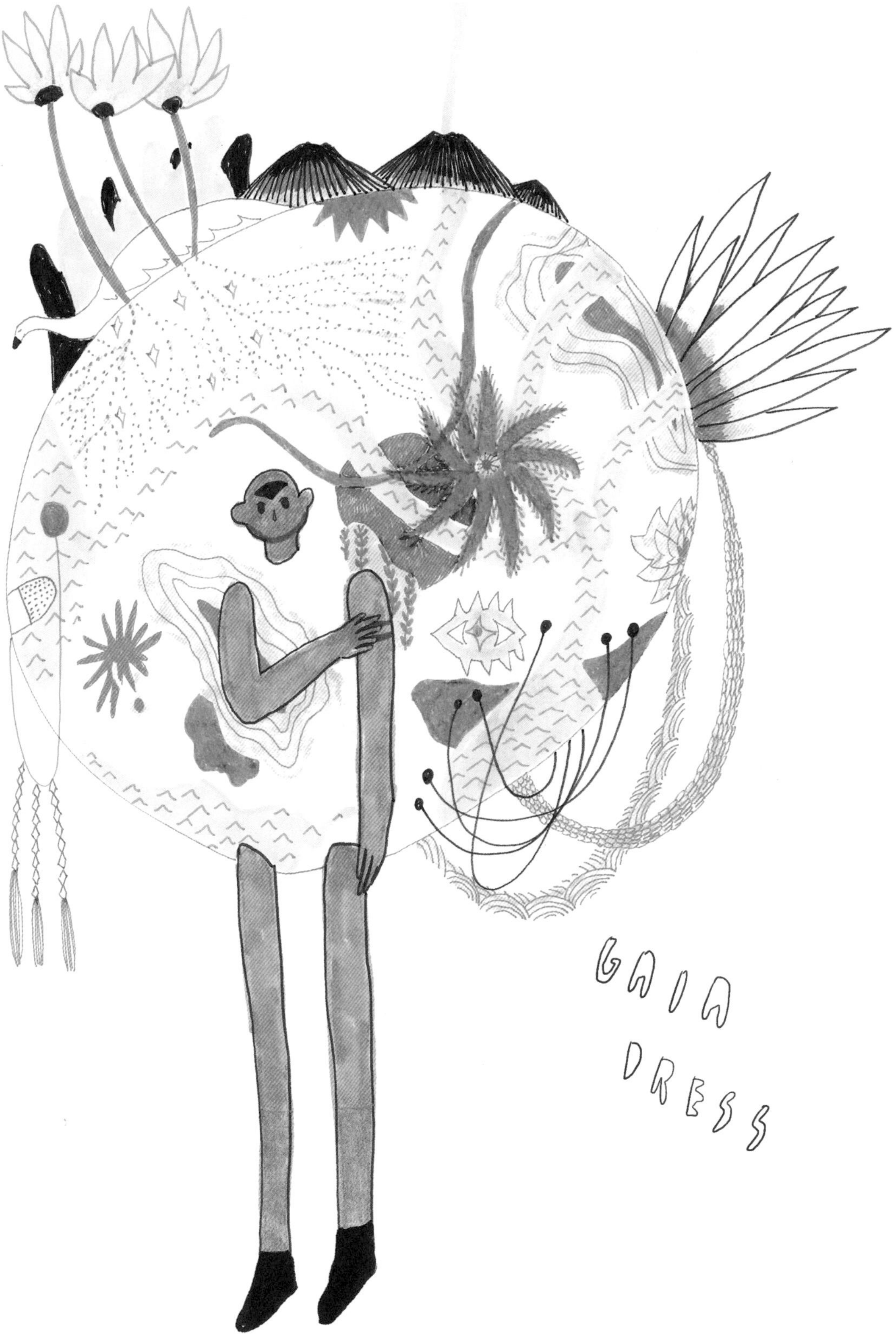
GAIA
DRESS

TERRARIUM TOP

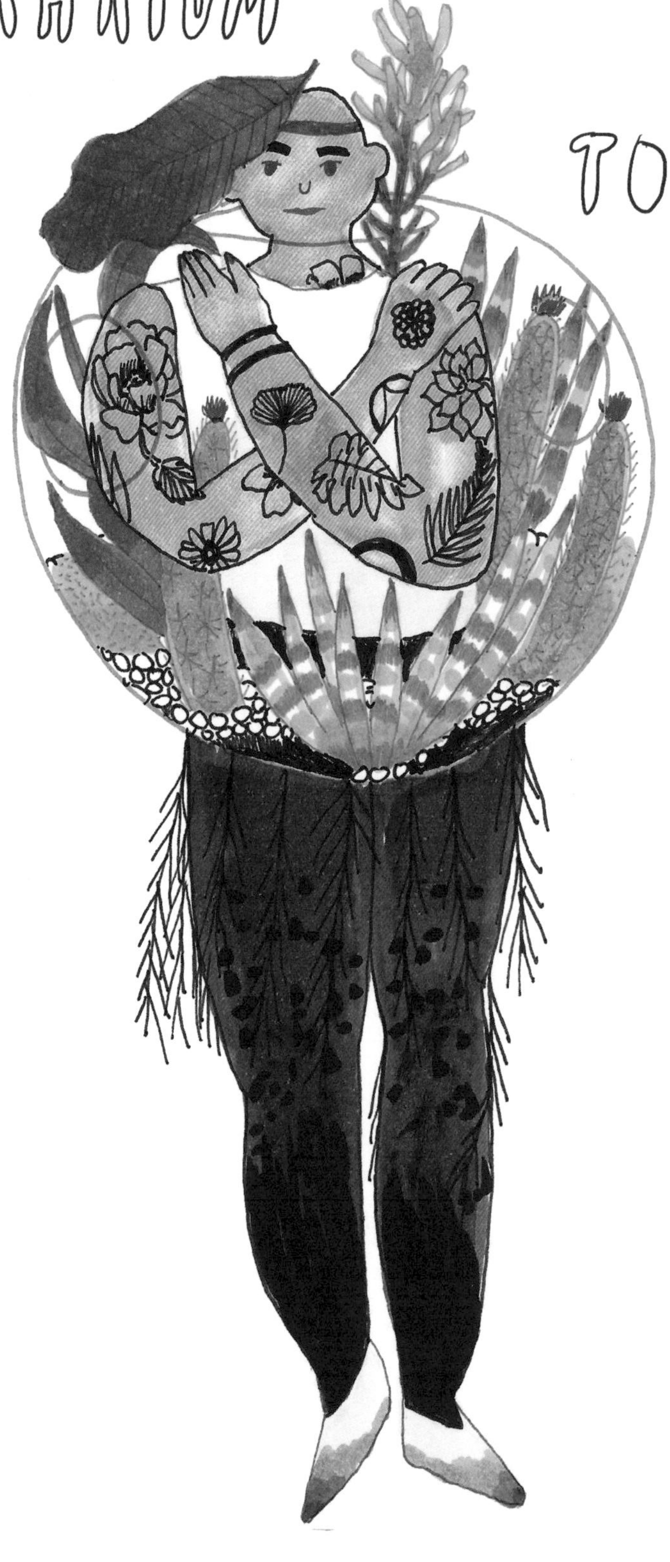

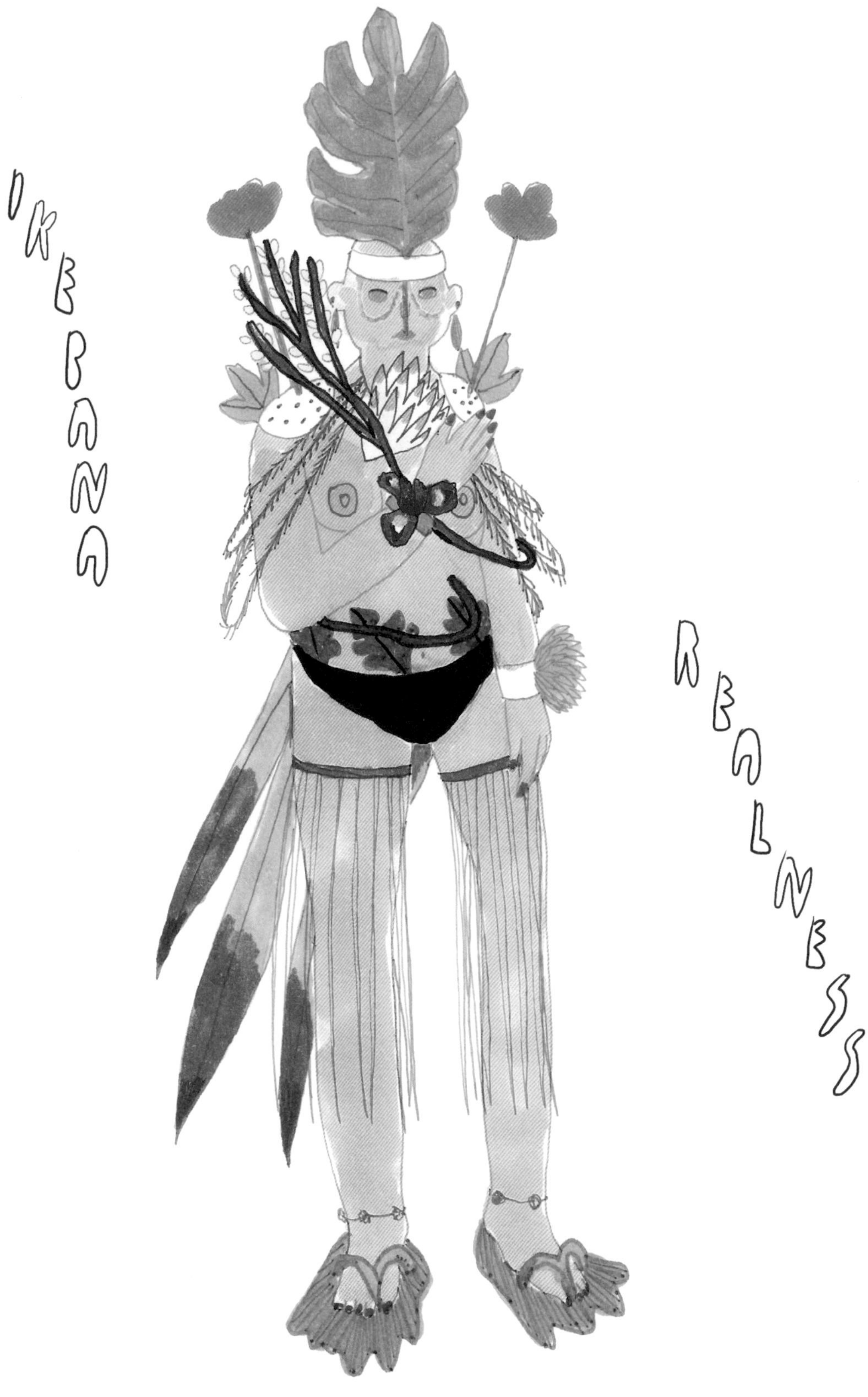
IKEBANA
REALNESS

SPIRITUALITY

MYTHOLOGY

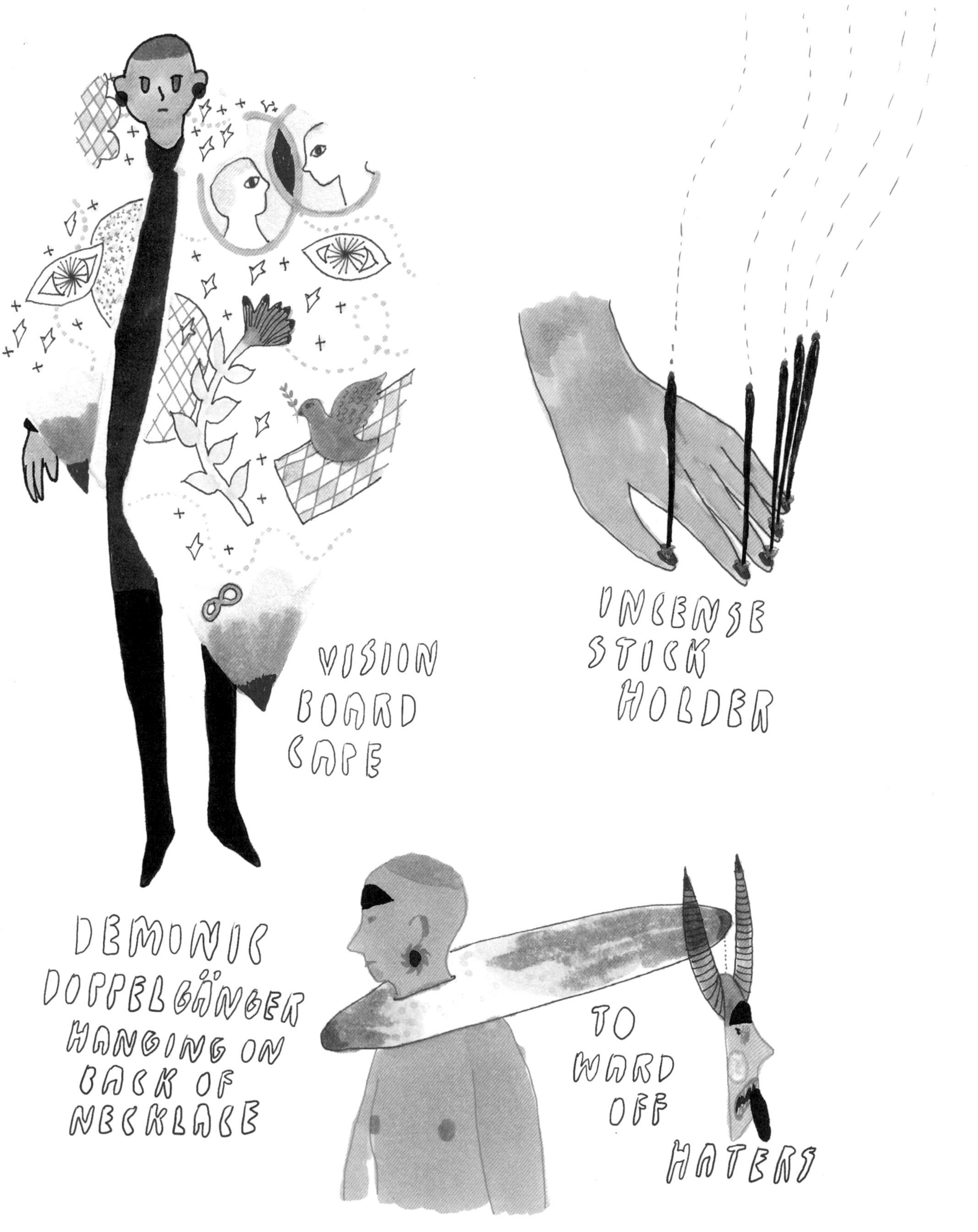
VISION BOARD CAPE
INCENSE STICK HOLDER
DEMONIC DOPPELGÄNGER HANGING ON BACK OF NECKLACE
TO WARD OFF HATERS

"NO MUD, NO LOTUS"
– THICH NHAT HANH

MUD
LOTUS
DRESS

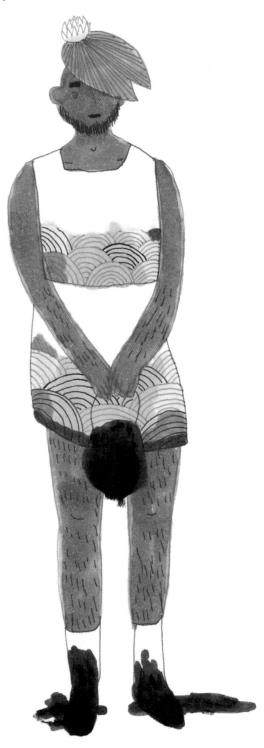

STAMPING ON
THE DEMON
OF YOUR
INSECURITIES
CEREMONIAL
DRESS

COMMUNITY

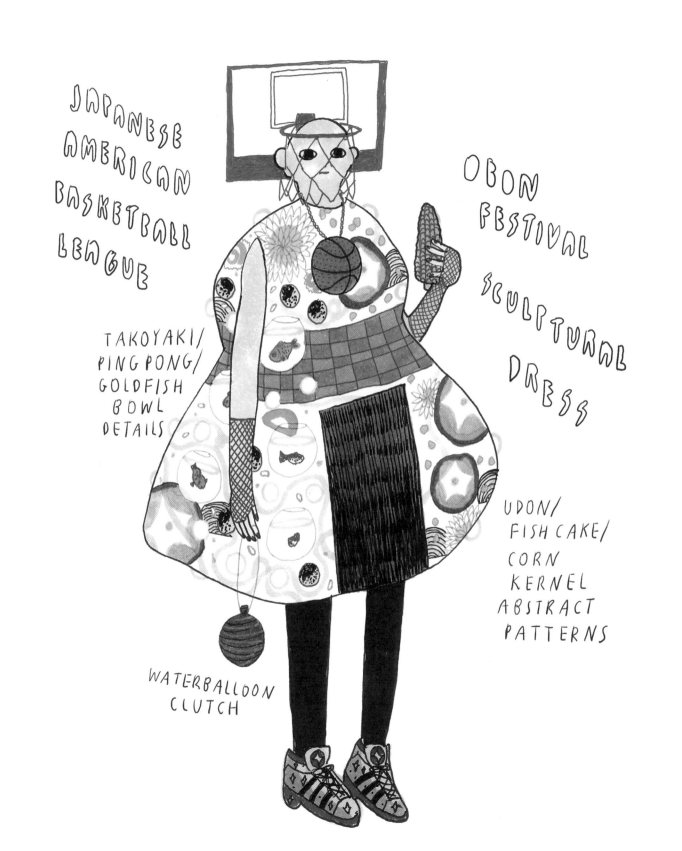

JAPANESE
AMERICAN
BASKETBALL
LEAGUE

OBON
FESTIVAL
SCULPTURAL
DRESS

TAKOYAKI/
PING PONG/
GOLDFISH
BOWL
DETAILS

UDON/
FISH CAKE/
CORN
KERNEL
ABSTRACT
PATTERNS

WATERBALLOON
CLUTCH

COMMUNITY CAPE: DIALOGUE

COMMUNAL PUBLIC CAPE WORN BY MINIMUM OF THREE PEOPLE TO ENCOURAGE DIALOGUE AND COMMUNITY INTERACTION.

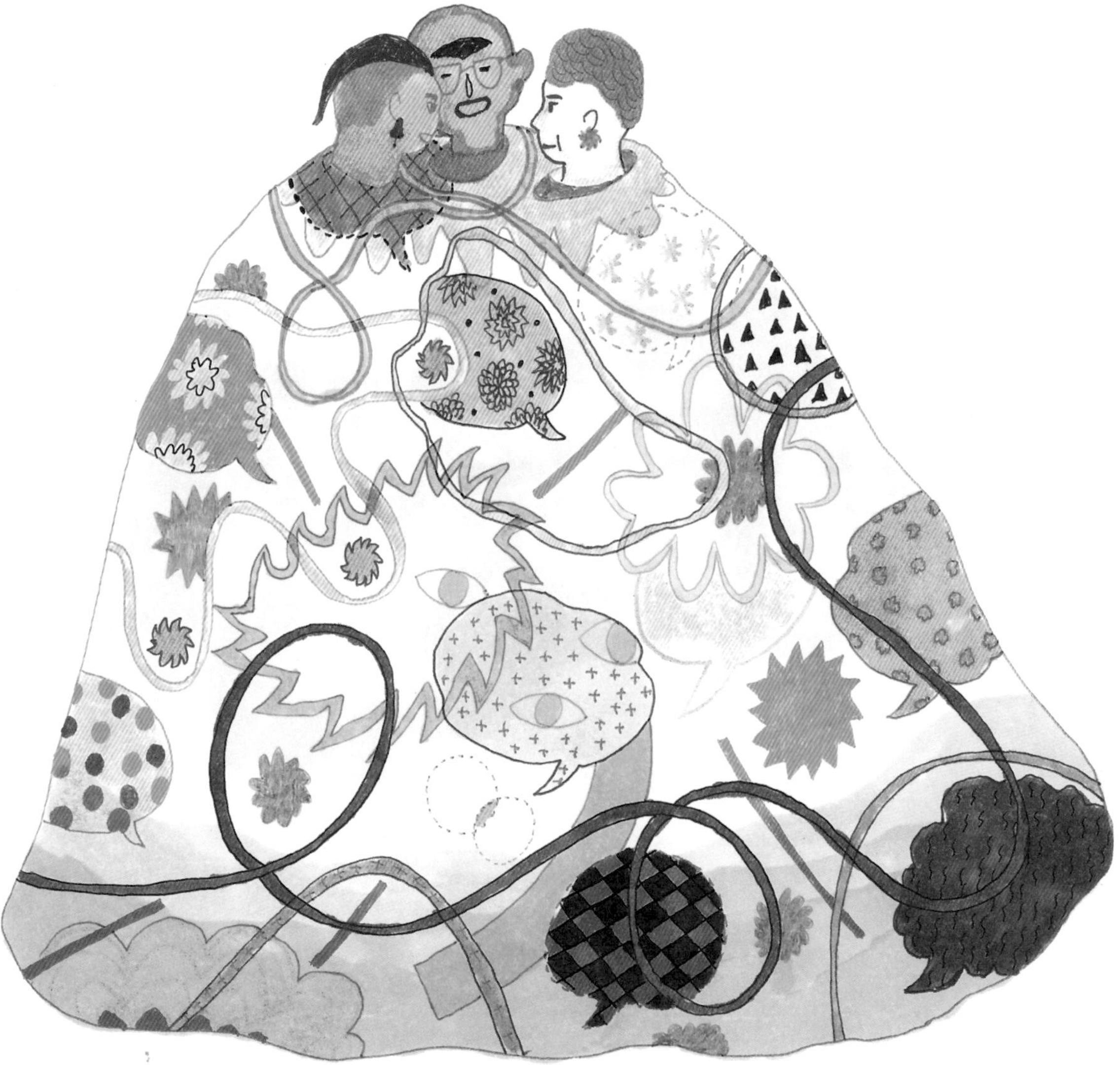

COMMUNITY CAPE: SILENCE

A PUBLIC COMMUNAL CAPE FOR STANDING IN REFLECTIVE, CONTEMPLATIVE SILENCE WITH FELLOW COMMUNITY MEMBERS.

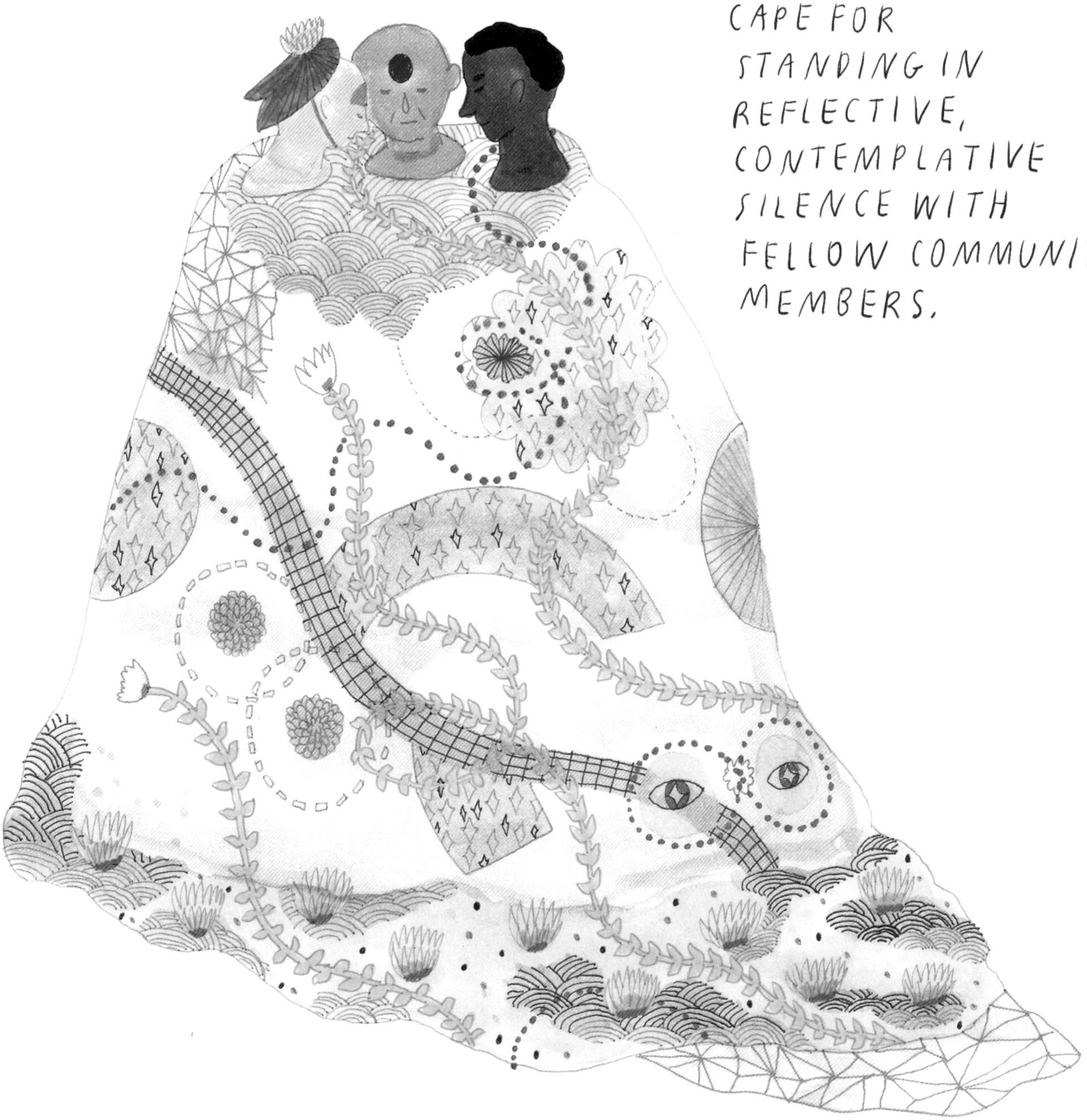

COMMUNITY NOTICE BOARD DRESS

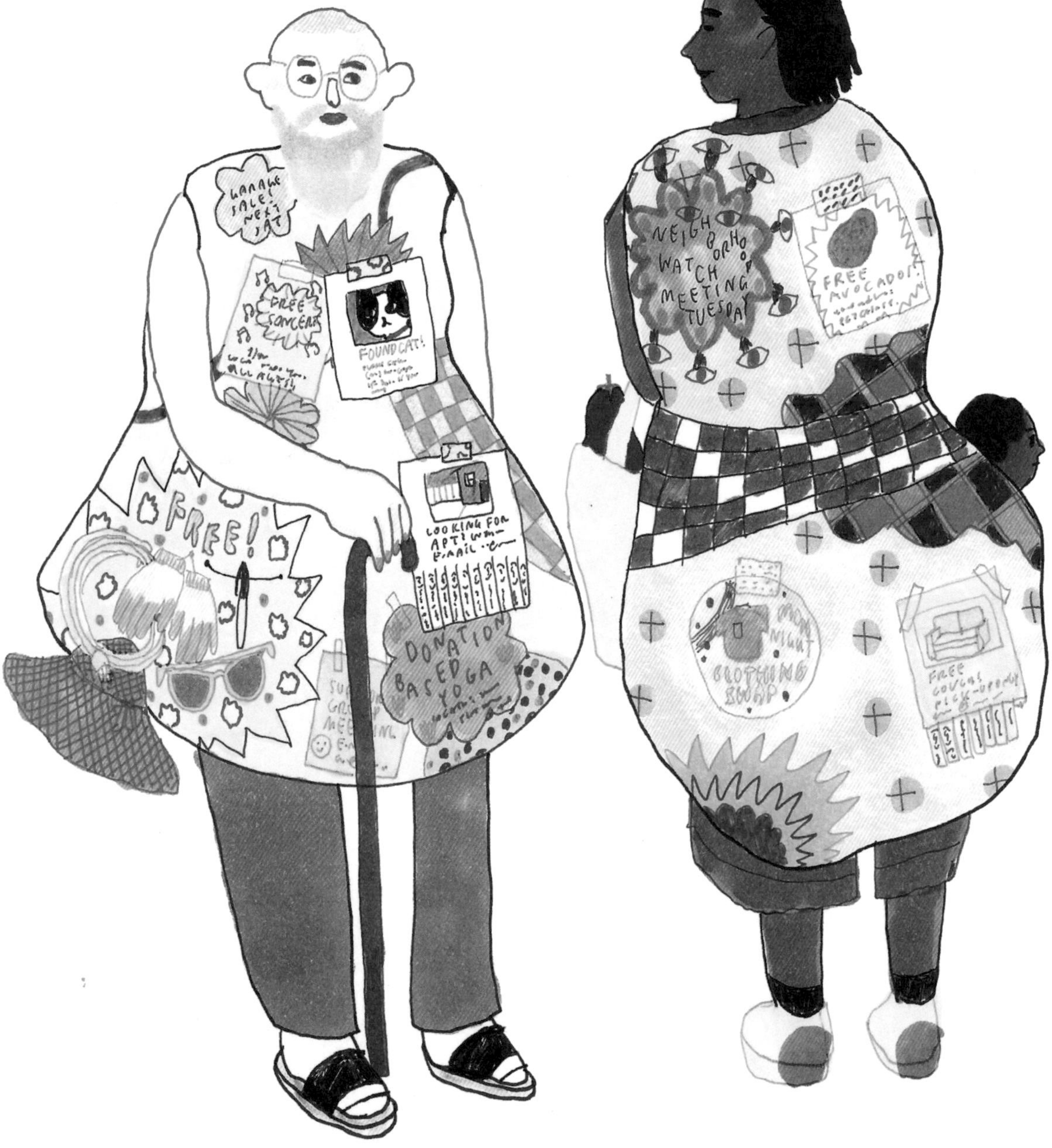
FREE CONCERT
FOUND CAT!
LOOKING FOR APT!
FREE!
DONATION BASED YOGA
NEIGHBORHOOD WATCH MEETING TUESDAY
FREE AVOCADOS!
CLOTHING SWAP

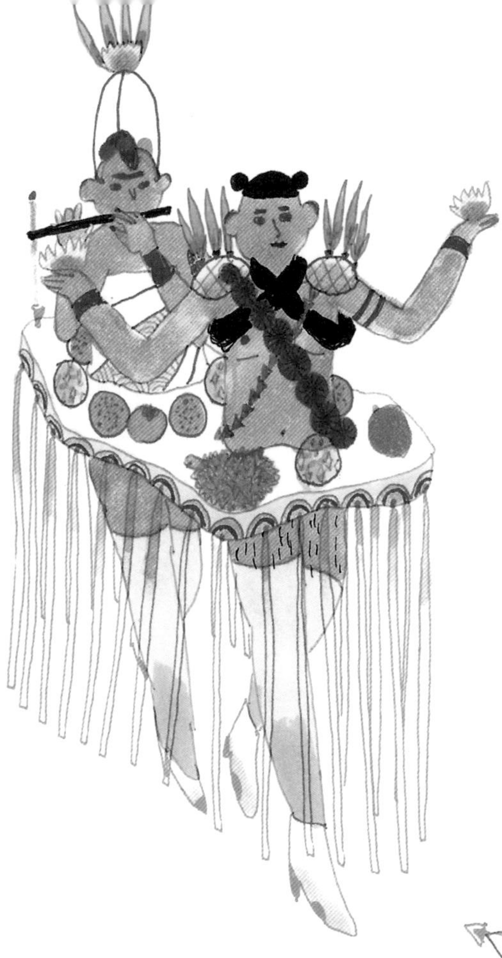

COMMUNITY PARADE FLOAT DRESS/OUTFIT

DRESS UP AS A CEREMONIAL PARADE FLOAT BY YOURSELF OR WITH OTHERS.

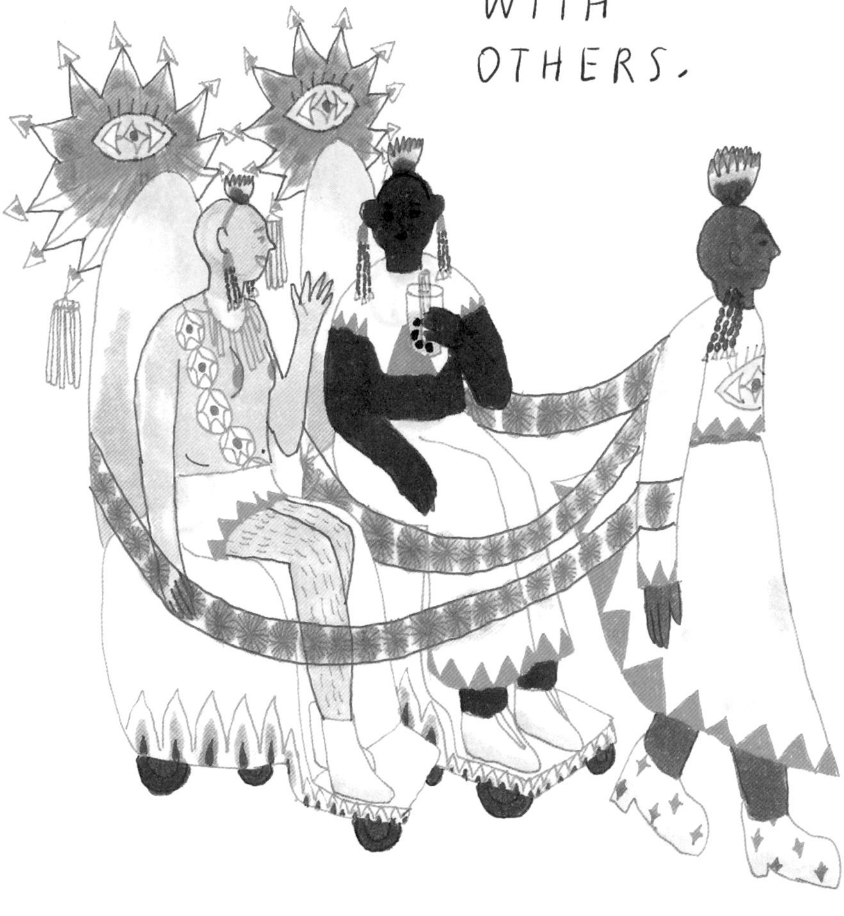

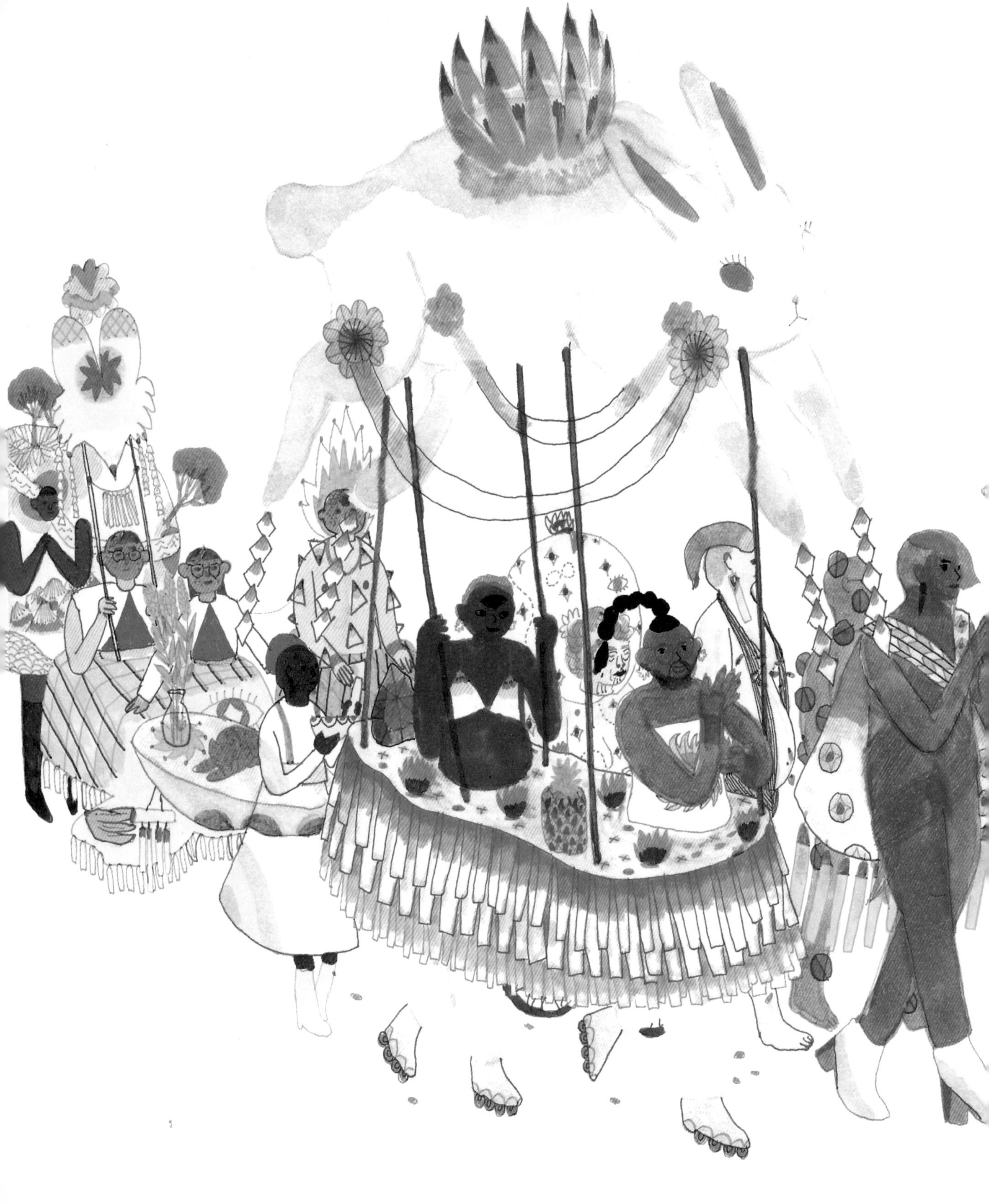

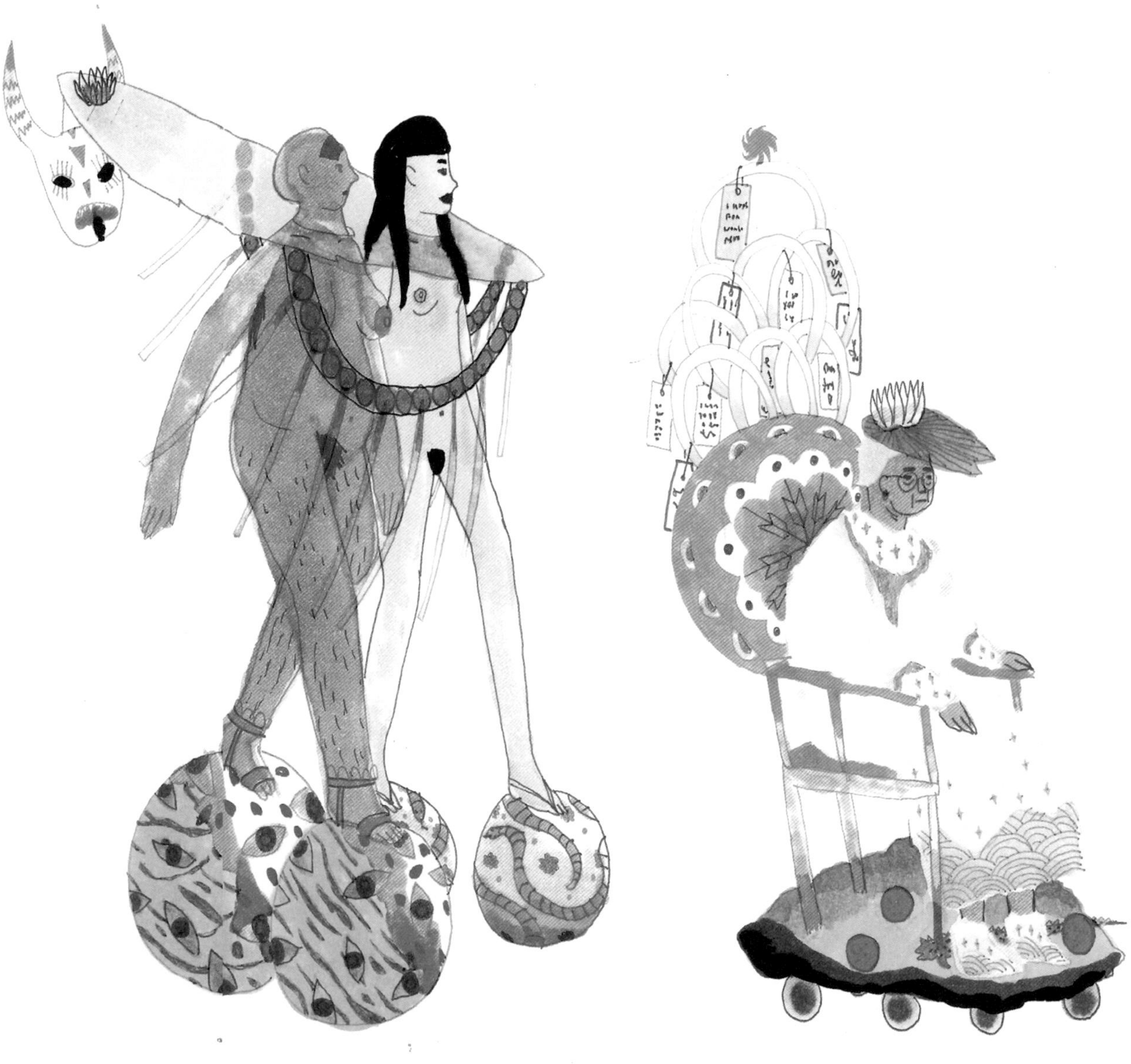

TECHNOLOGY

FUTURE

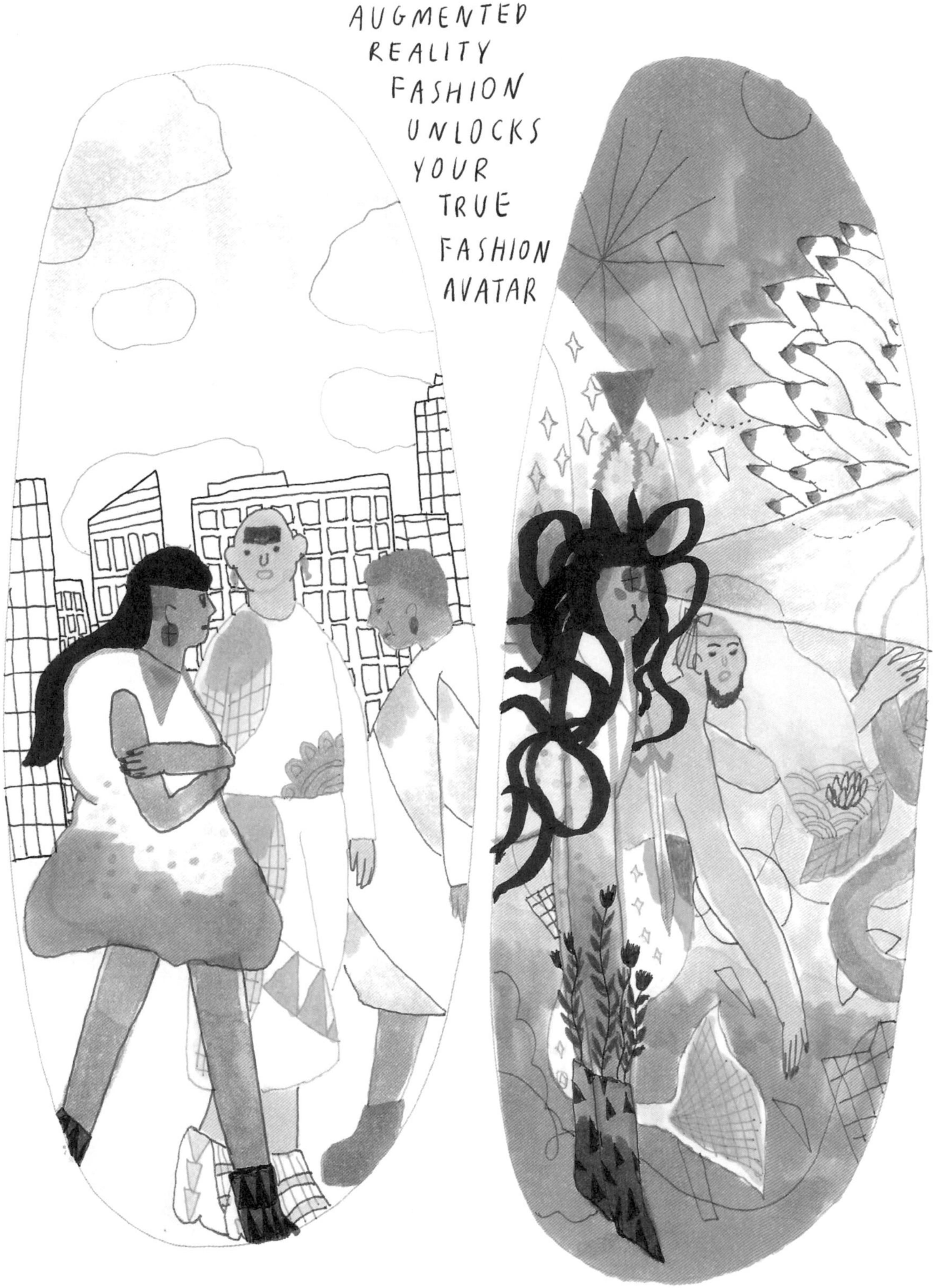
AUGMENTED
REALITY
FASHION
UNLOCKS
YOUR
TRUE
FASHION
AVATAR

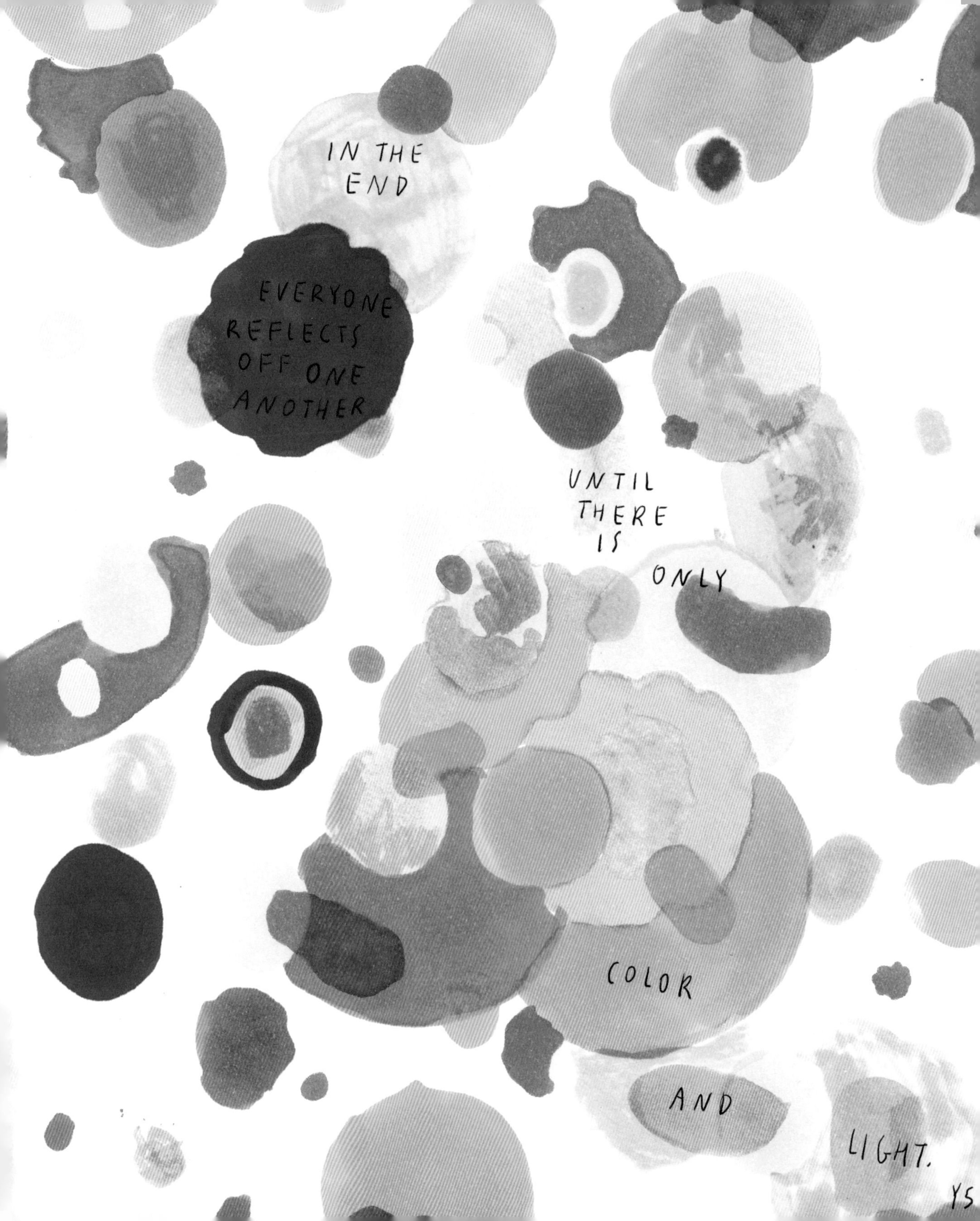
IN THE END
EVERYONE REFLECTS OFF ONE ANOTHER
UNTIL THERE IS ONLY
COLOR
AND
LIGHT.
YS

yumisakugawa •••

[redacted]
(SHAVED)
THIS HAIRCUT
THIS HAIRDO
CROCHETED EAR SLEEVES
STICK-ON FACE JEWELRY
COLORED DOTS ON NOSE/ EYEBROWS
CRYSTAL-STUDDED BODY SUIT
HOLES CUT OUT TO EXPOSE BOOBS, AUREOLAS AND NIPPLES COVERED BY SUNBURST-SHAPE OF FABRIC
BLACK TEETH
CROTCH-HIGH BOOTS

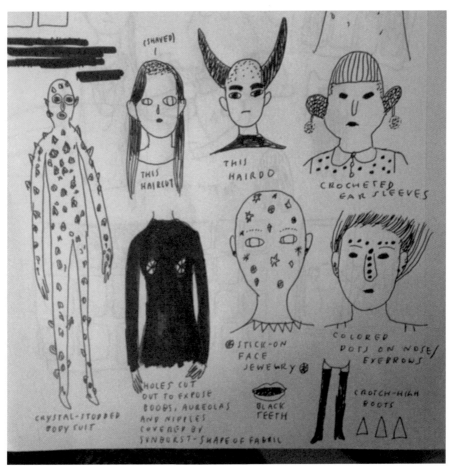

Liked by **tinypyramid**, **wangstagram** and **184 others**

yumisakugawa More fashion predictions from a non-fashion person 👯 👯 👯

View all 6 comments

JULY 3, 2014

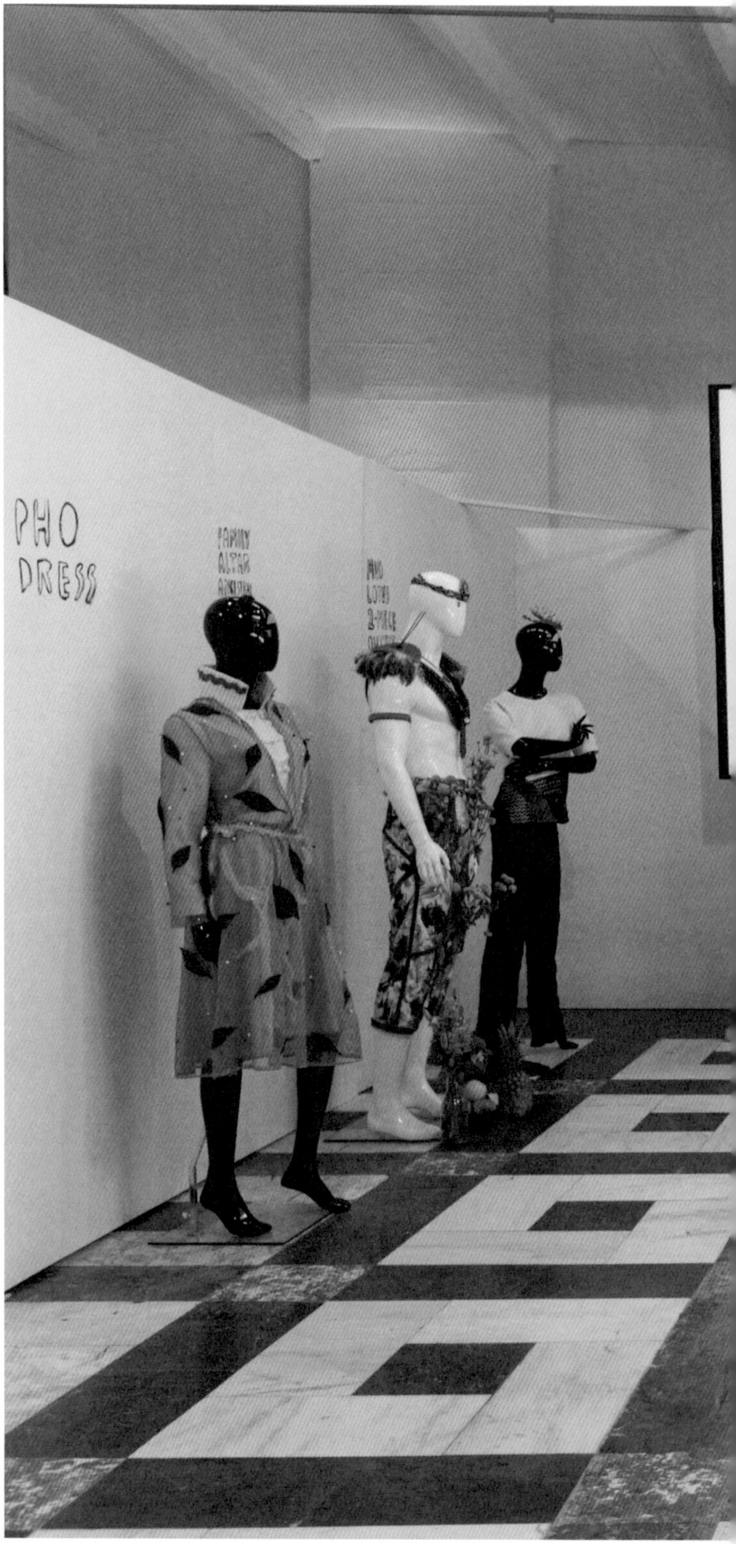
PHO
DRESS
FAMILY
ALTAR

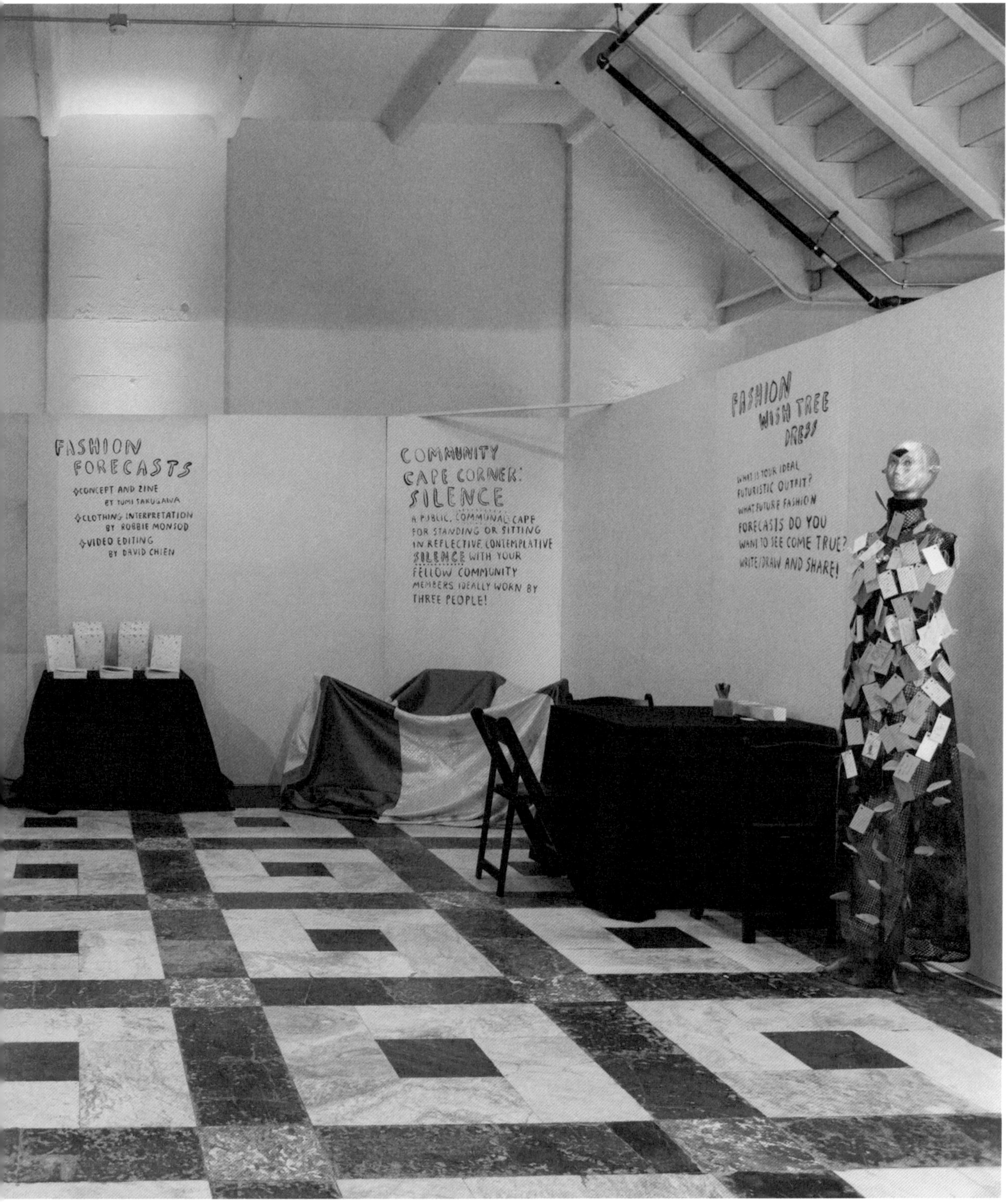
FASHION FORECASTS
CONCEPT AND ZINE BY YUMI SAKUGAWA
CLOTHING INTERPRETATION BY ROBBIE MONSOD
VIDEO EDITING BY DAVID CHIEN
COMMUNITY CAPE CORNER: SILENCE
A PUBLIC, COMMUNAL CAPE FOR STANDING OR SITTING IN REFLECTIVE, CONTEMPLATIVE SILENCE WITH YOUR FELLOW COMMUNITY MEMBERS IDEALLY WORN BY THREE PEOPLE!
FASHION WISH TREE DRESS
WHAT IS YOUR IDEAL FUTURISTIC OUTFIT? WHAT FUTURE FASHION FORECASTS DO YOU WANT TO SEE COME TRUE? WRITE/DRAW AND SHARE!

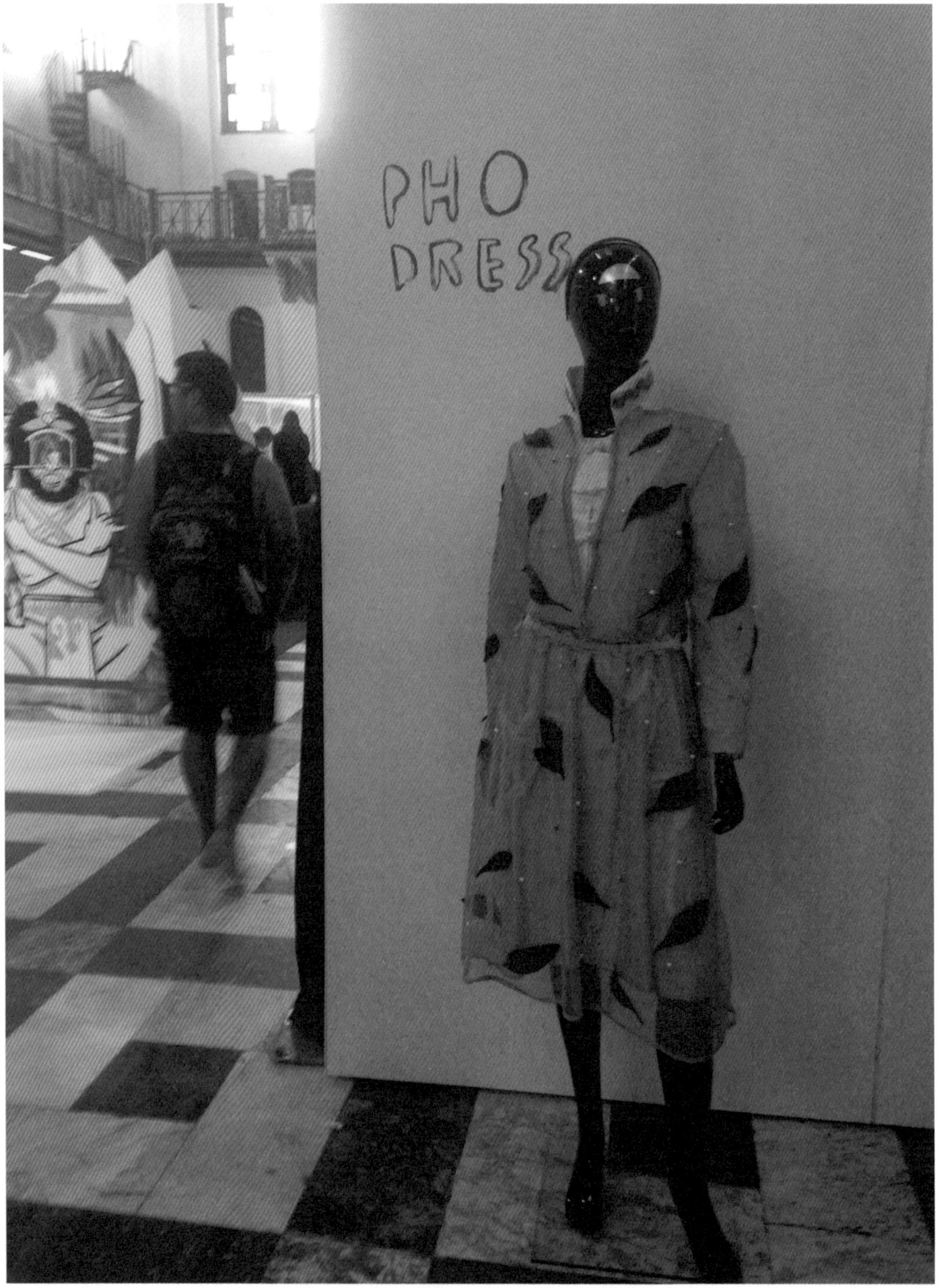
PHO
DRESS

FAMILY
ALTAR
ANCESTRAL
WORSHIP
CEREMONIAL
EVERYDAY
WEAR

MUD
LOTUS
2-PIEC
OUTF

"NO MUD,
NO LOTUS"
- THICH NHAT HA

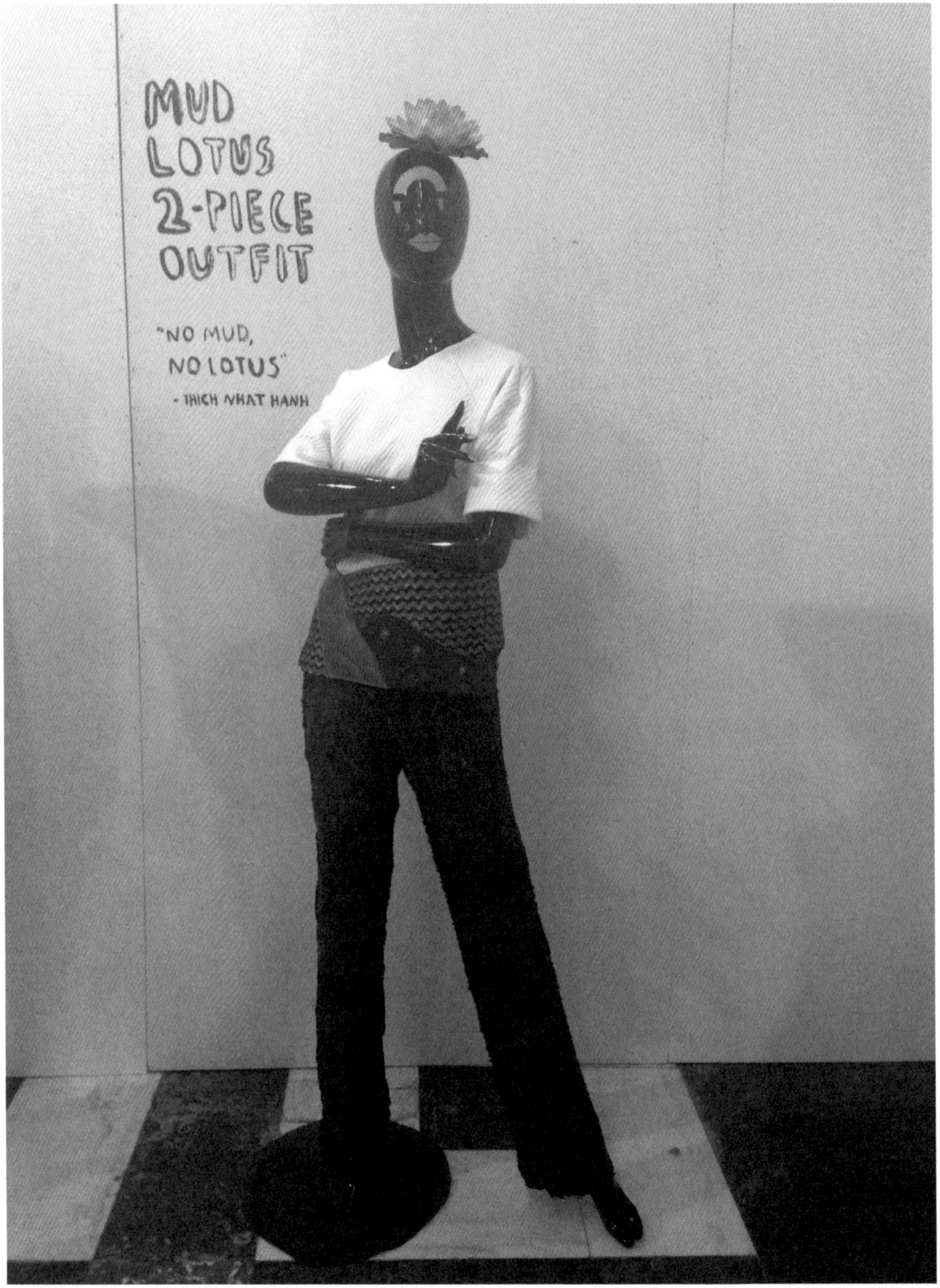
MUD
LOTUS
2-PIECE
OUTFIT
"NO MUD,
NO LOTUS"
- THICH NHAT HANH

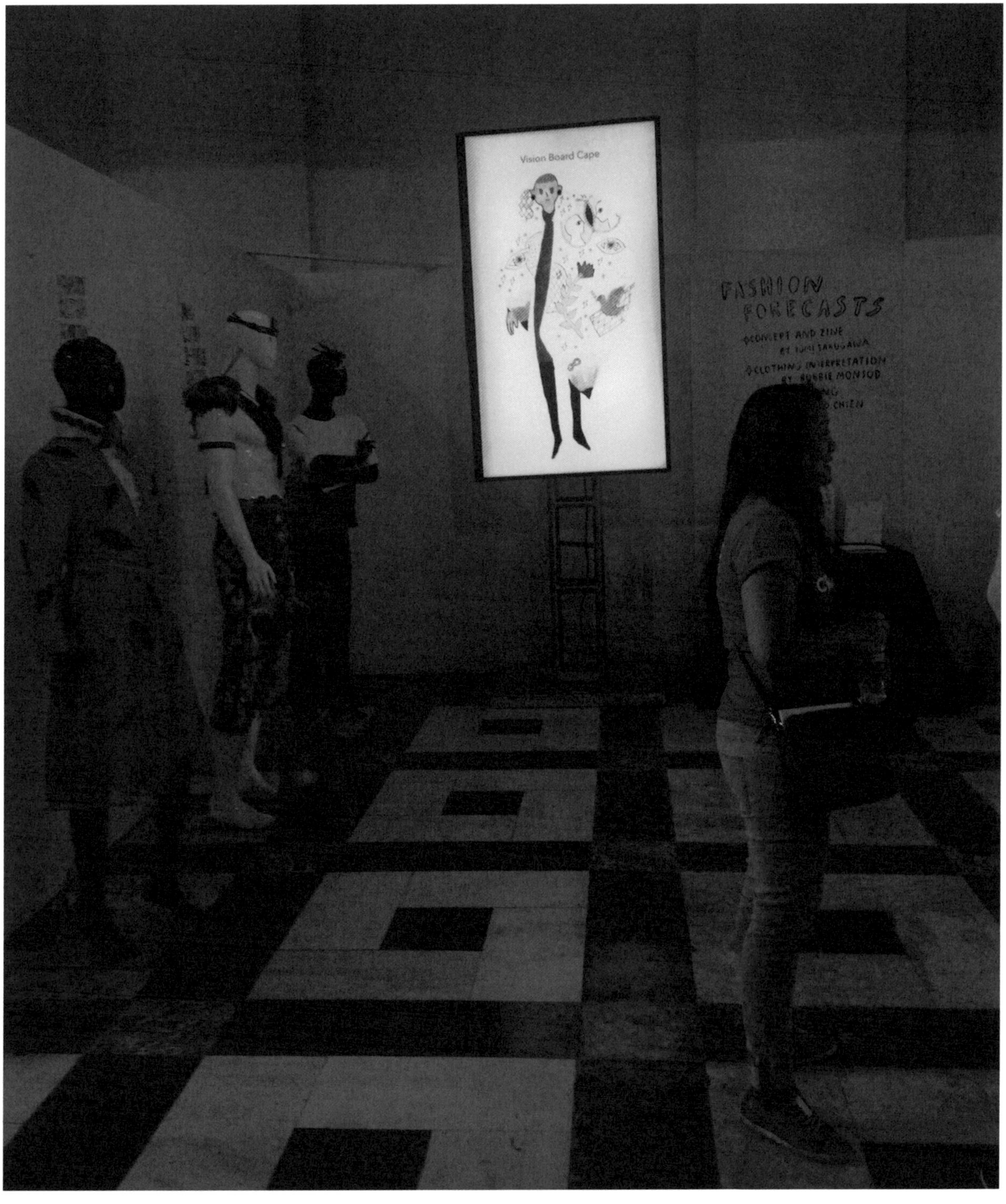

Vision Board Cape
FASHION FORECASTS
CONCEPT AND ZINE
CLOTHING INTERPRETATION

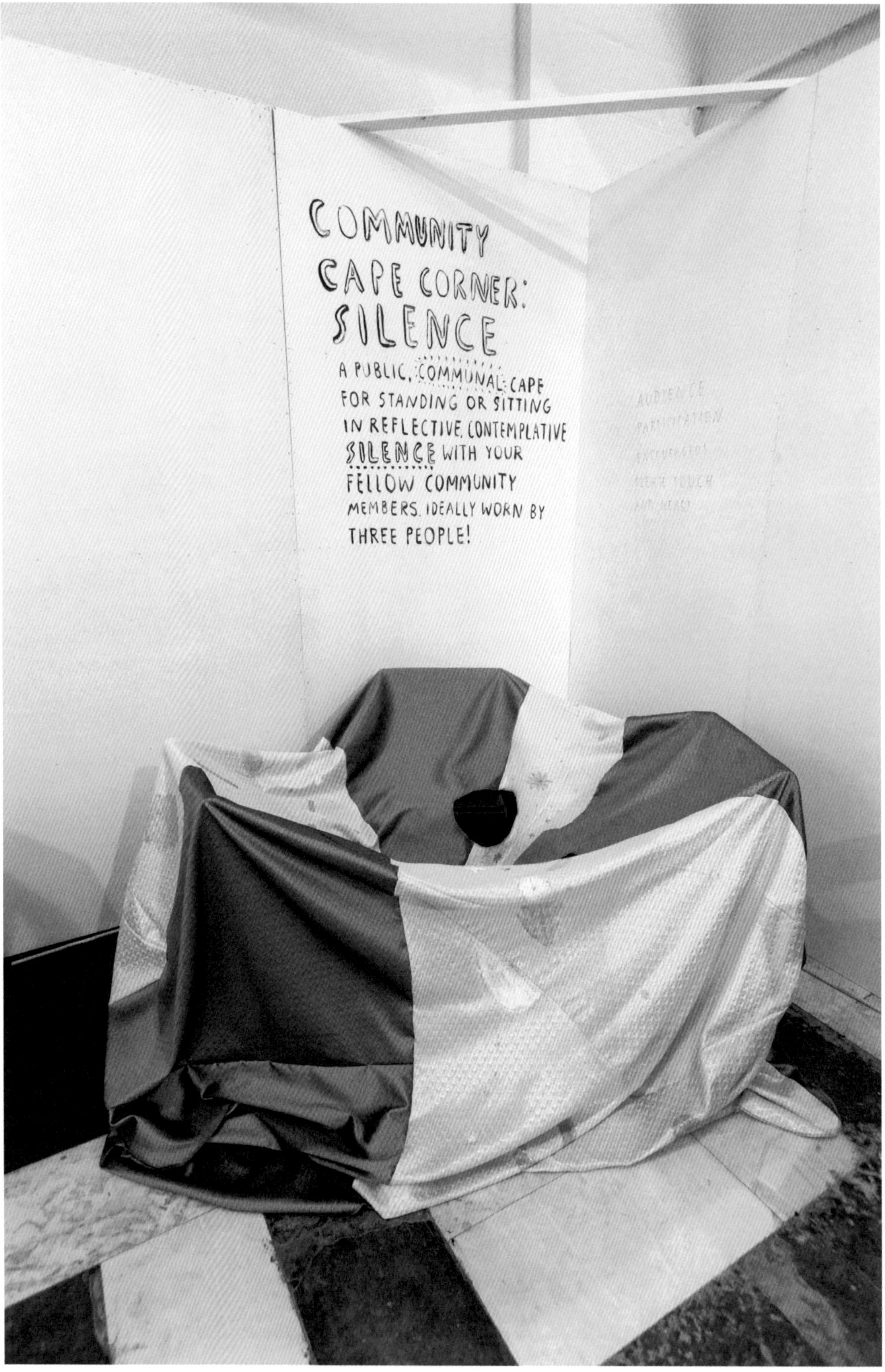
COMMUNITY
CAPE CORNER:
SILENCE
A PUBLIC, COMMUNAL CAPE
FOR STANDING OR SITTING
IN REFLECTIVE, CONTEMPLATIVE
SILENCE WITH YOUR
FELLOW COMMUNITY
MEMBERS. IDEALLY WORN BY
THREE PEOPLE!

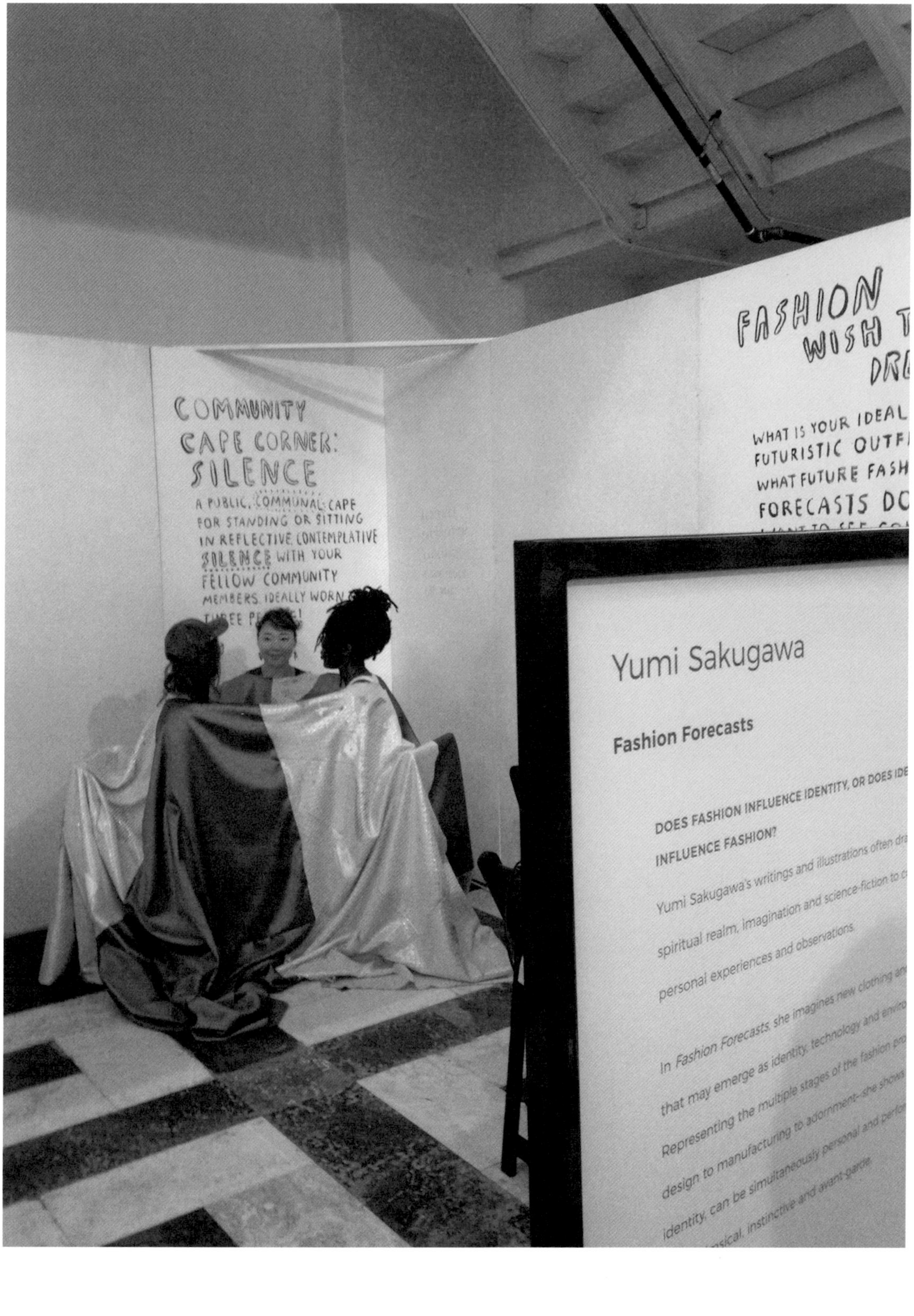
COMMUNITY
CAPE CORNER:
SILENCE
A PUBLIC, COMMUNAL CAPE
FOR STANDING OR SITTING
IN REFLECTIVE CONTEMPLATIVE
SILENCE WITH YOUR
FELLOW COMMUNITY
MEMBERS. IDEALLY WORN
FASHION
WHAT IS YOUR IDEAL
FUTURISTIC
WHAT FUTURE
FORECASTS
Yumi Sakugawa
Fashion Forecasts
DOES FASHION INFLUENCE IDENTITY, OR DOES
INFLUENCE FASHION?
Yumi Sakugawa's writings and illustrations often
spiritual realm, imagination and science-fiction to
personal experiences and observations.
In Fashion Forecasts, she imagines new clothing
that may emerge as identity, technology and
Representing the multiple stages of the fashion
design to manufacturing to adornment—she shows
identity, can be simultaneously personal and
instinctive and avant-garde.

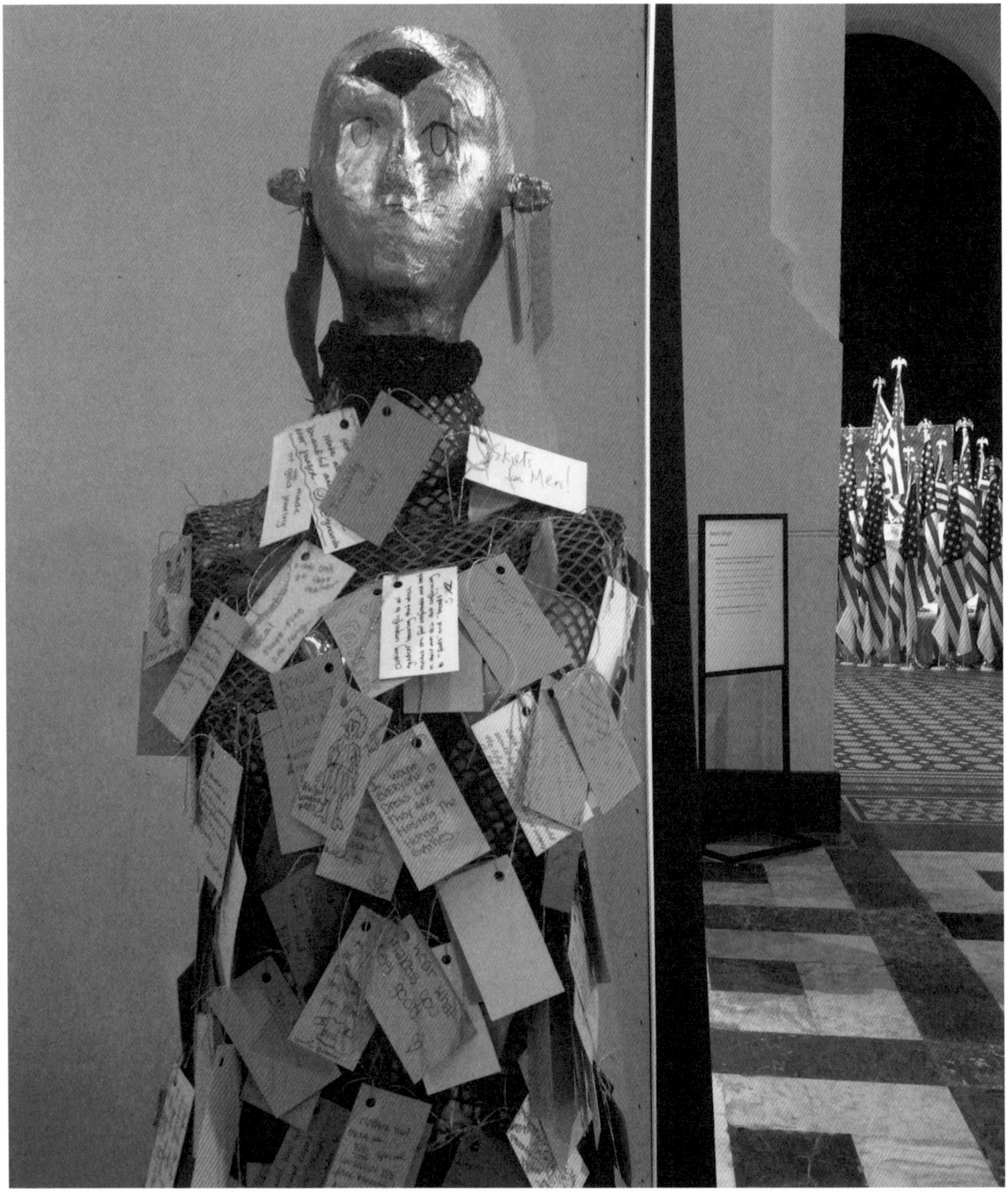
Skirts for Men!
Where EVERYONE Dresses like They ARE Hosting The Hunger Games

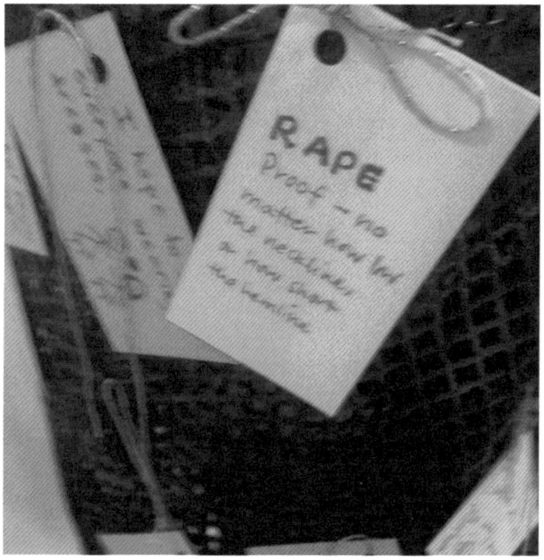
RAPE
Proof – no

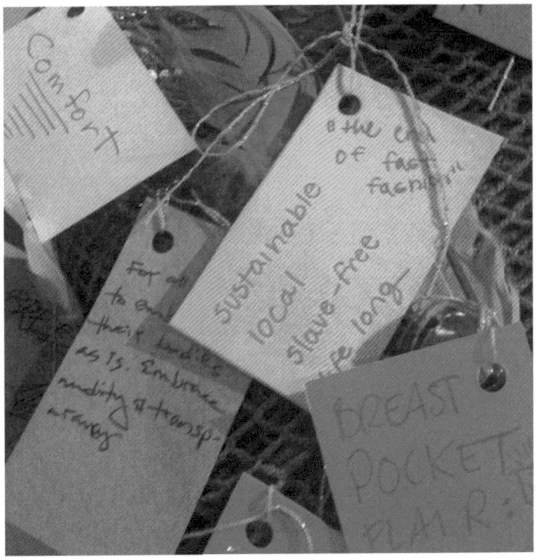
Comfort
Sustainable
local
slave-free
BREAST
POCKET

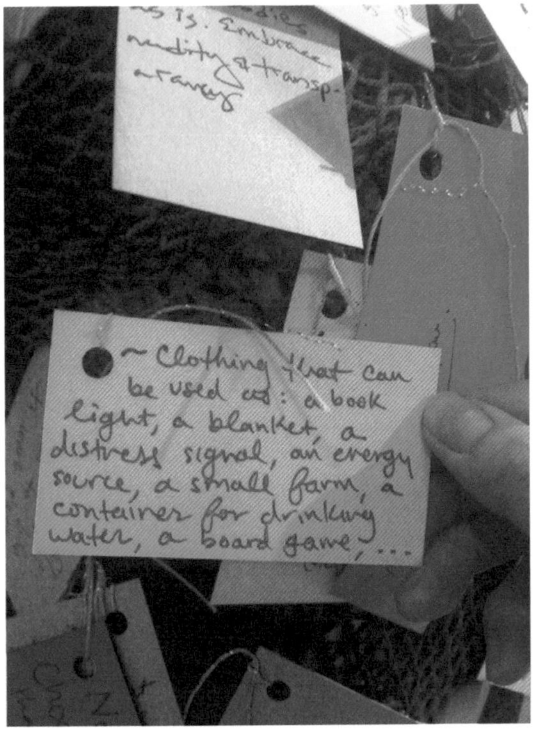
~ Clothing that can be used as: a book light, a blanket, a distress signal, an energy source, a small farm, a container for drinking water, a board game, ...

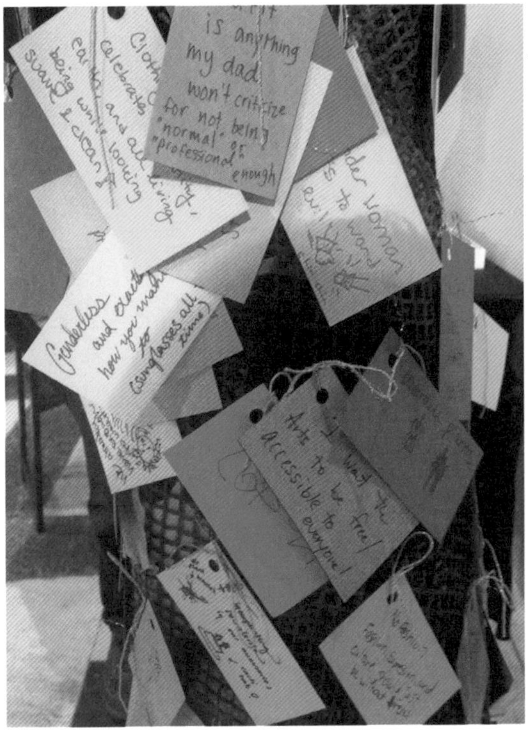
is anything my dad won't criticize for not being "normal" or "professional" enough
Genderless and exactly how you want to
Art to be free/ Accessible to everyone!

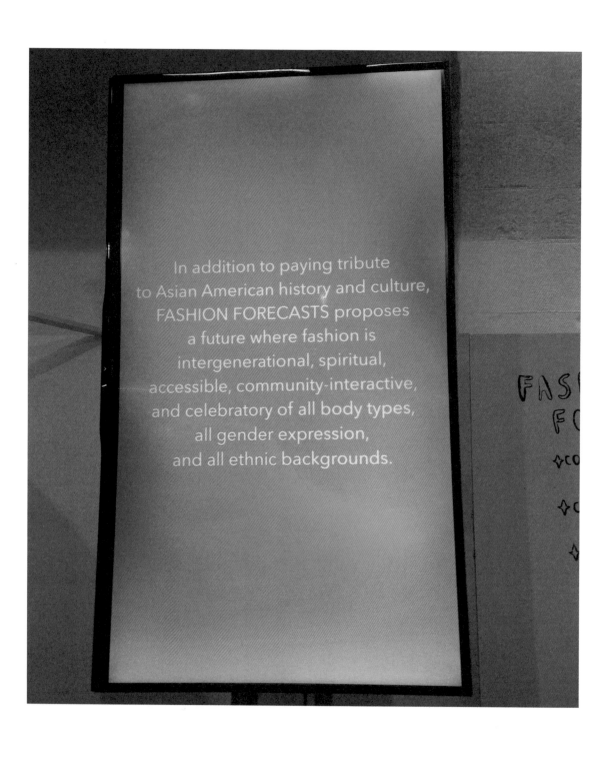

In addition to paying tribute
to Asian American history and culture,
FASHION FORECASTS proposes
a future where fashion is
intergenerational, spiritual,
accessible, community-interactive,
and celebratory of all body types,
all gender expression,
and all ethnic backgrounds.

yumisakugawa ...

GEOMETRIC UNIBROW
UNIBROW OMBRE HAIR
FISH DRESS
SPHERICAL DRESS
???
BAC(K)CESSORY
KITE EARRINGS

Liked by **tinypyramid**, **aparnapkin** and **539 others**

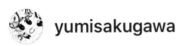

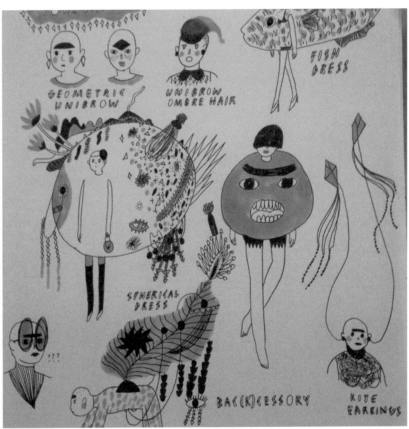

yumisakugawa FASHION FORECASTS

View all 16 comments

OCTOBER 25, 2015

FASHION ADVICE

✦ TIP: MAKE SURE YOUR CLOTHES REALLY FIT YOU. IF CLOTHING ITEM IS LOOSE FITTING OR "OFF," CONSIDER GETTING IT TAILORED, IT MAKES A HUGE DIFFERENCE!

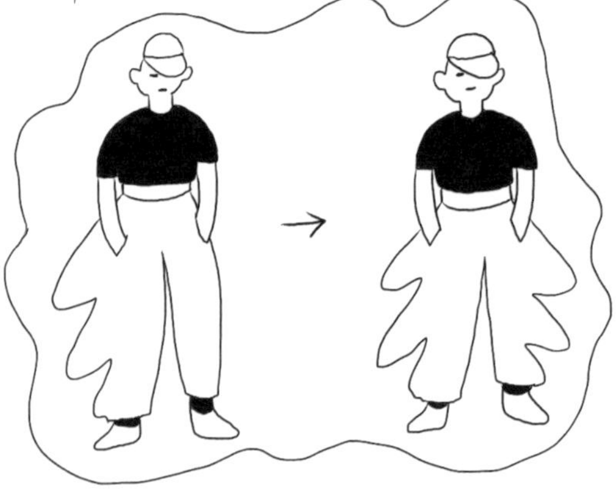

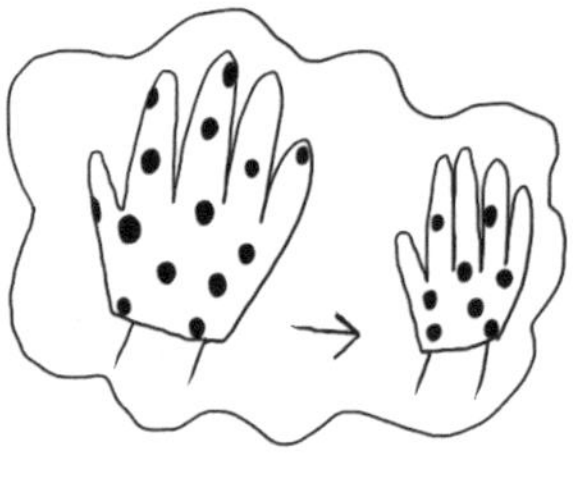

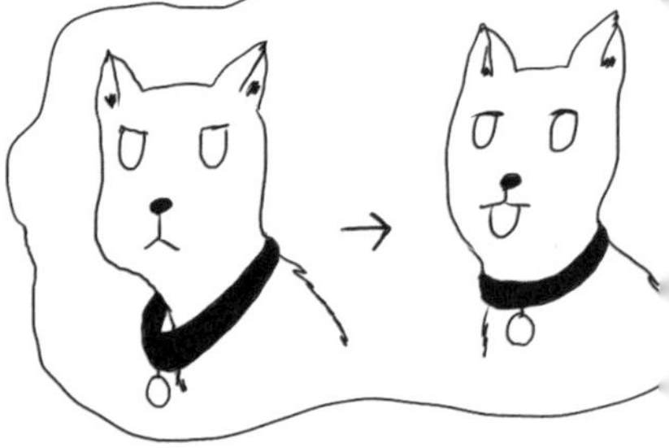

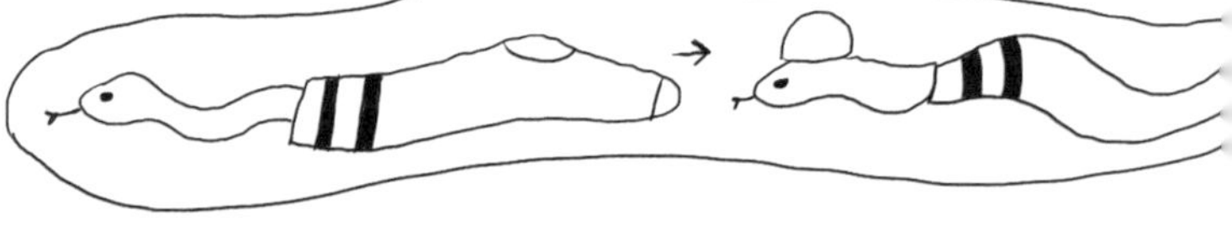

✦ FEELING "BLAH" AND BORED BY YOUR FASHION CHOICES? MIX UP YOUR SILHOUETTES WHEN YOU BUY CLOTHES AND STYLE YOURSELF.

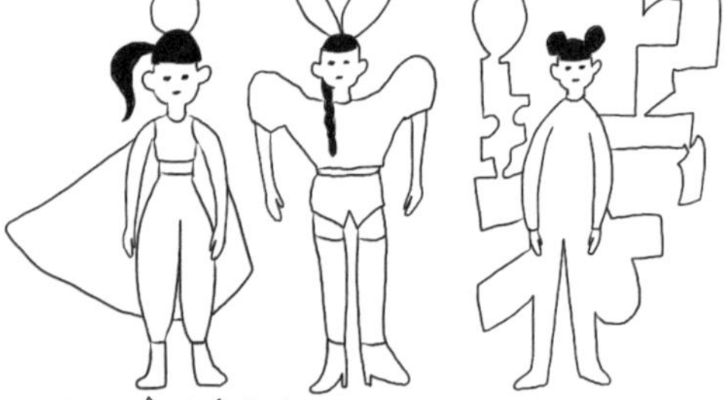

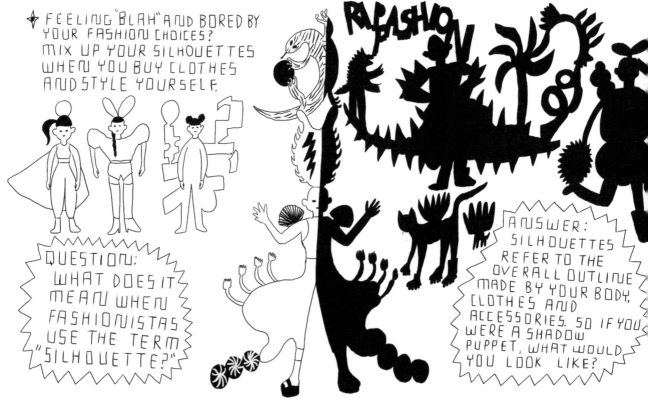

QUESTION: WHAT DOES IT MEAN WHEN FASHIONISTAS USE THE TERM "SILHOUETTE?"

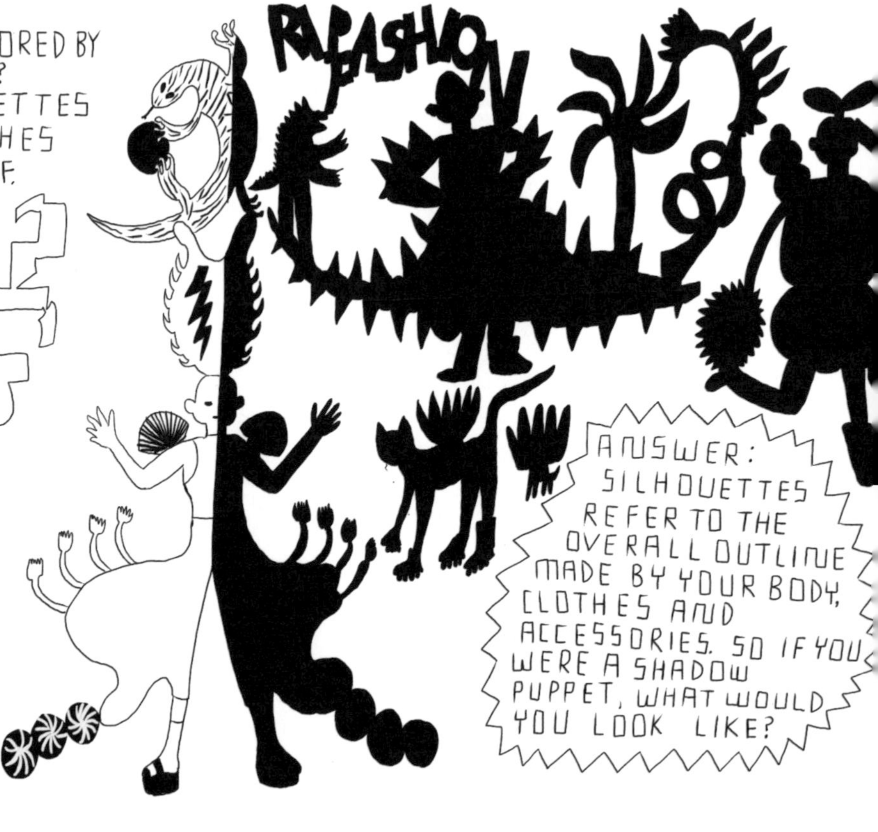

ANSWER: SILHOUETTES REFER TO THE OVERALL OUTLINE MADE BY YOUR BODY, CLOTHES AND ACCESSORIES. SO IF YOU WERE A SHADOW PUPPET, WHAT WOULD YOU LOOK LIKE?

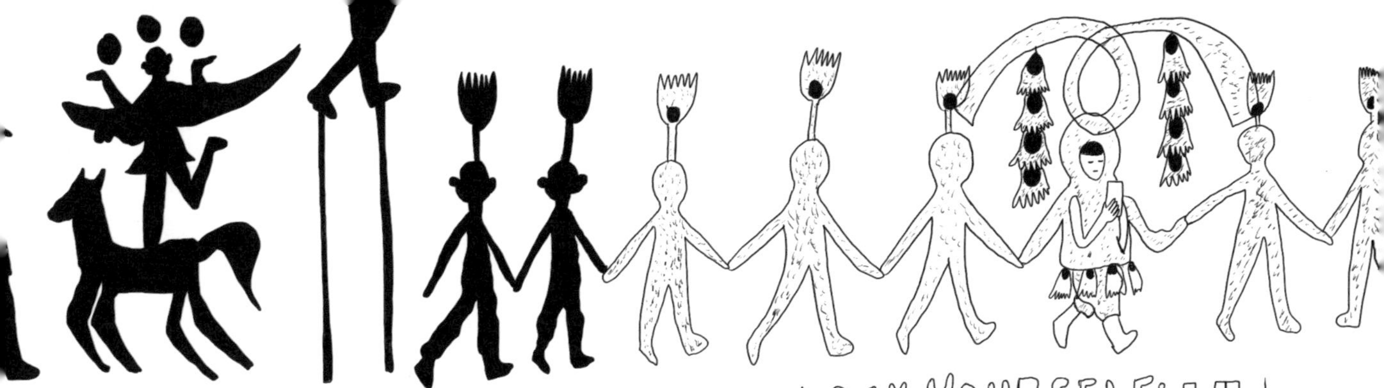

✧ TIP: BE AWARE OF WHERE SYMBOLS, STYLES, AND IMAGES COME FROM, AND THE CULTURAL/HISTORICAL CONTEXT OF HOW THEY ARE USED. OTHERWISE, YOU MIGHT COME ACROSS AS A CLUELESS JERK.

✧ ASK YOURSELF: AM I BEING A "FASHION QUESTION" OR A "FASHION STATEMENT"? BE A FASHION STATEMENT.

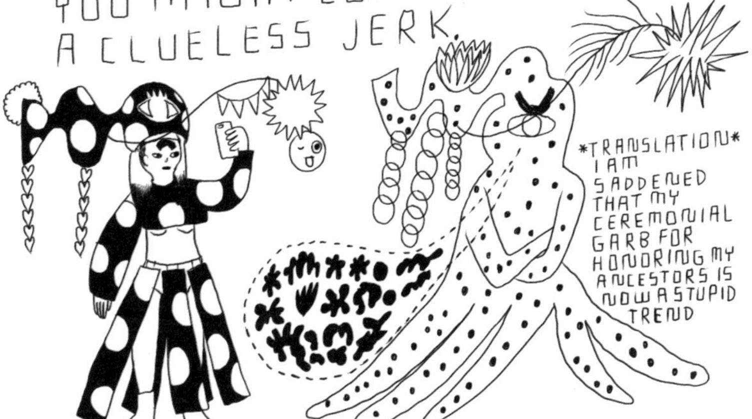

TRANSLATION I AM SADDENED THAT MY CEREMONIAL GARB FOR HONORING MY ANCESTORS IS NOW A STUPID TREND

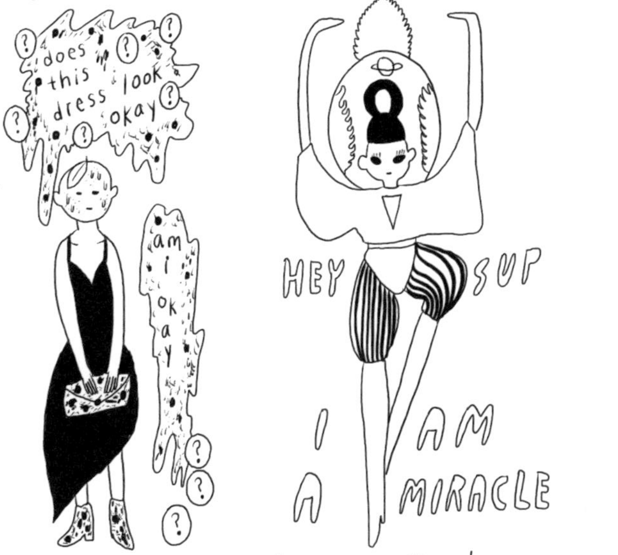

does this dress look okay
am i okay
HEY SUP
I AM A MIRACLE

✧ CHOOSE ONE DETAIL YOU WANT TO REALLY DRAW ATTENTION TO AND EMPHASIZE IT FOR DRAMATIC EFFECT. LIKE THIS STATEMENT NECKLACE.*

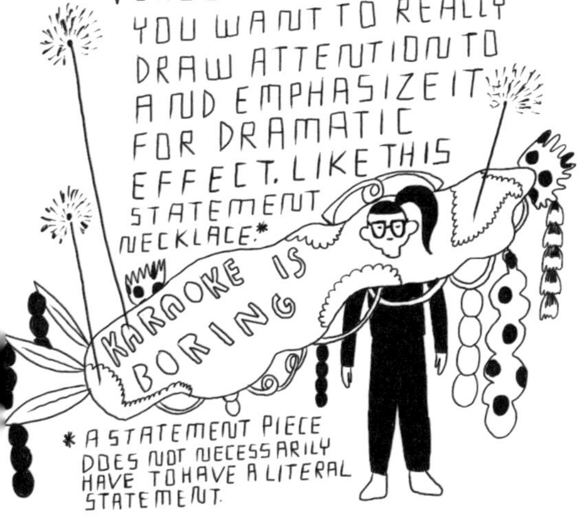

KARAOKE IS BORING

* A STATEMENT PIECE DOES NOT NECESSARILY HAVE TO HAVE A LITERAL STATEMENT.

✧ KNOW THE RULES SO YOU CAN BREAK THEM!

EXAMPLE: NIPPLE EXPOSURE = BAD

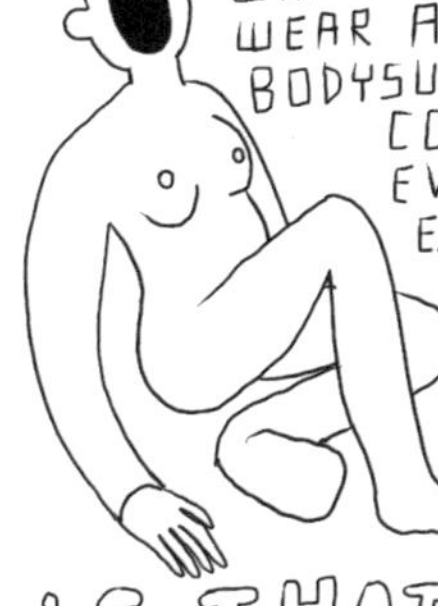

WHAT IF YOU WEAR A FULL (NIPPLE-COLORED) BODYSUIT THAT COVERS EVERYTHING EXCEPT FOR TWO VERY SMALL CUTOUT CIRCLES EXPOSING JUST YOUR NIPPLES?

IS THAT A CRIME?

EXAMPLE: PUBIC HAIR SHOULD NEVER BE SEEN.

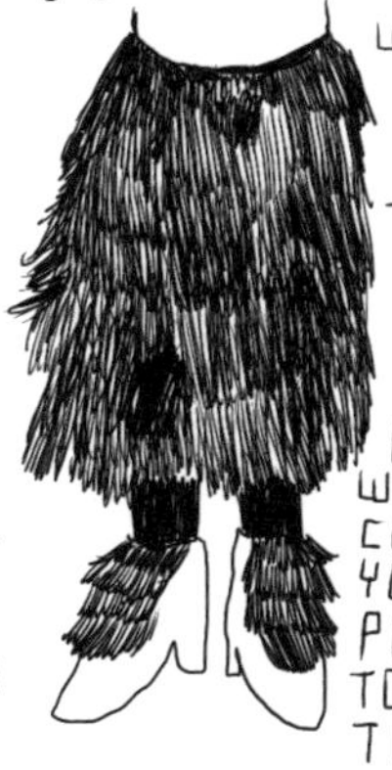

WHAT IF YOU WORE A FURRY SKIRT IN THE EXACT TEXTURE OF YOUR PUBIC MOUND AND THERE WAS A HOLE CUT OUT FOR YOUR REAL PUBIC HAIR TO POKE THROUGH?

FASHION FORECASTS THAT DID NOT MAKE IT INTO THE ORIGINAL ZINE

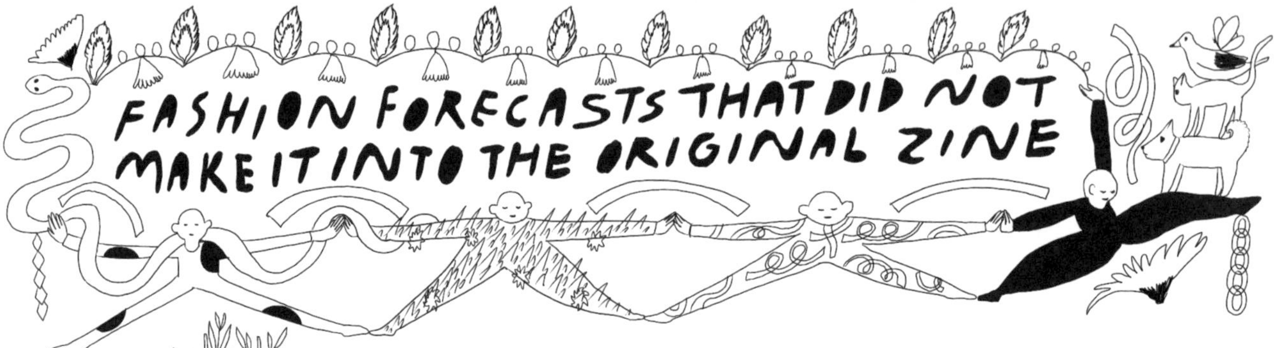

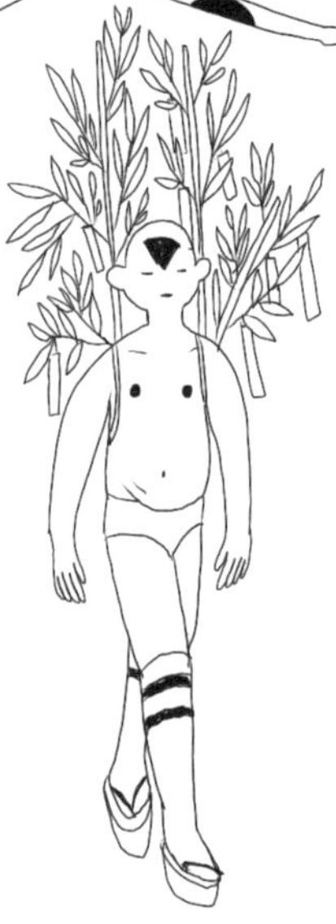

◊ WISH TREE

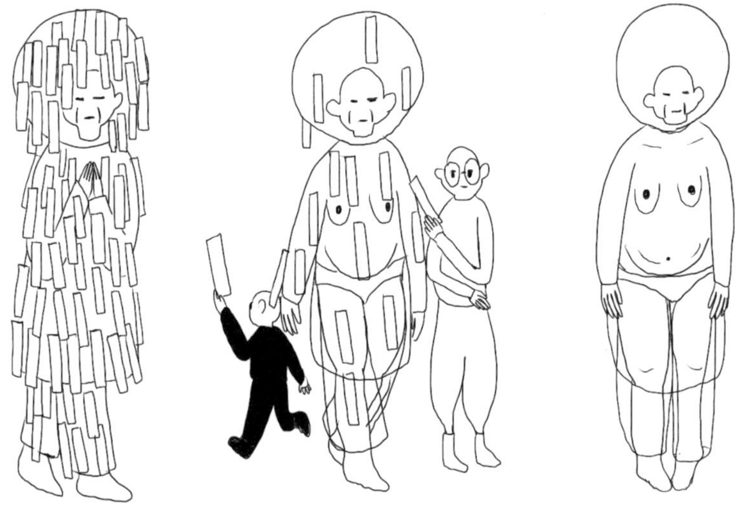

◊ GOOD FORTUNES DRESS - WEAR AN OUTFIT COVERED IN PAPER BLESSINGS. PASSER BYS TAKE A FORTUNE UNTIL THEY ARE ALL GONE.

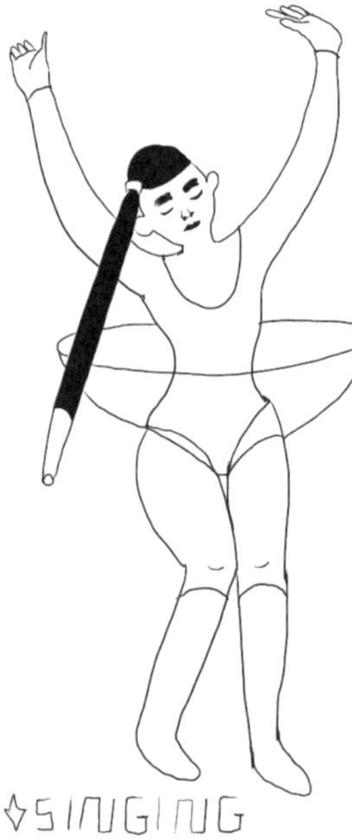

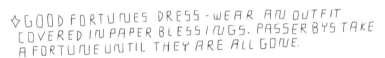

◊ SINGING BOWL SKIRT

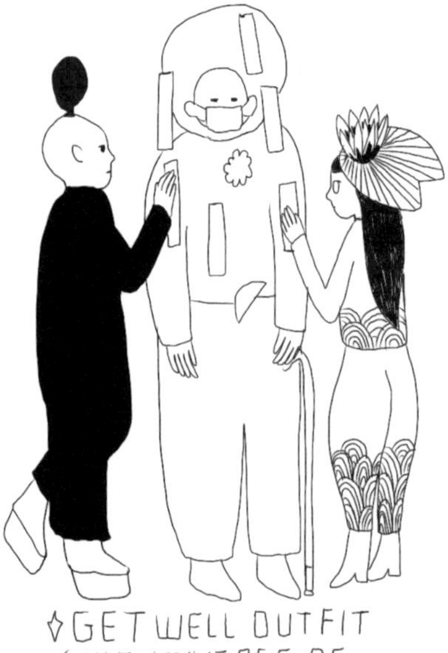

◊ GET WELL OUTFIT (THE INVERSE OF THE GOOD FORTUNES DRESS)

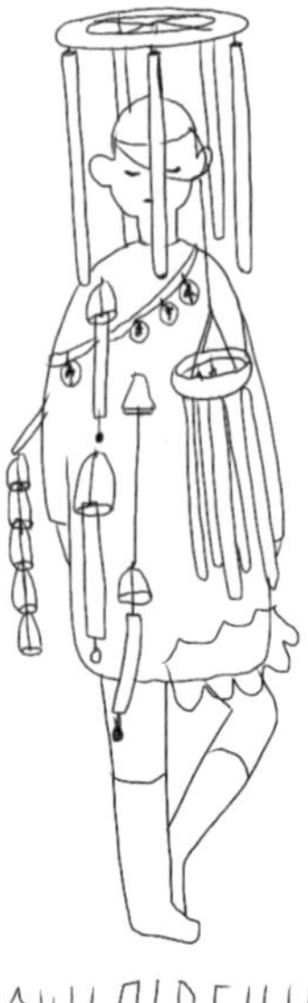

◊ WINDCHIME DRESS

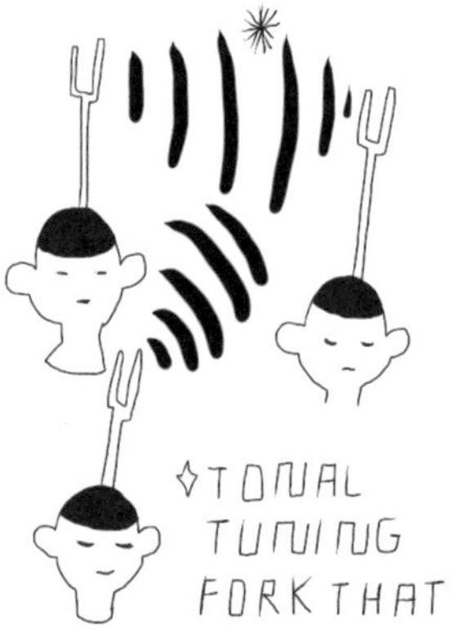

◊ TONAL TUNING FORK THAT CAN ONLY BE ACTIVATED IN COMPLETE MEDITATIVE SILENCE IN THE PRESENCE OF OTHERS

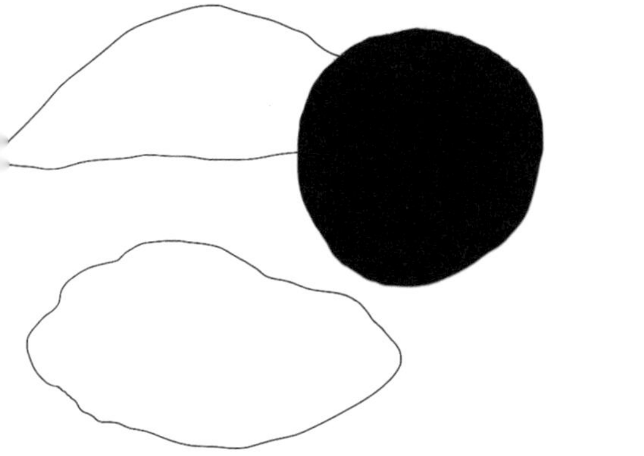

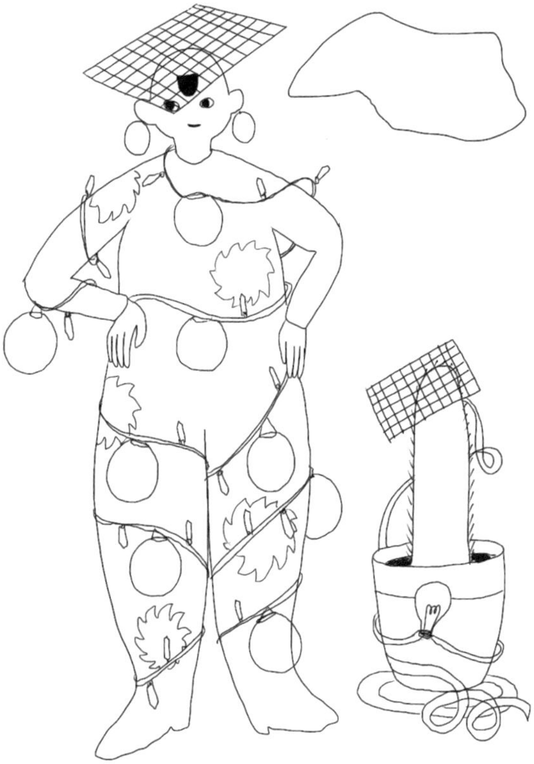

◊ SOLAR PANEL HEADPIECE AND ACCOMPANYING OUTFIT LIT UP BY ELECTRICITY

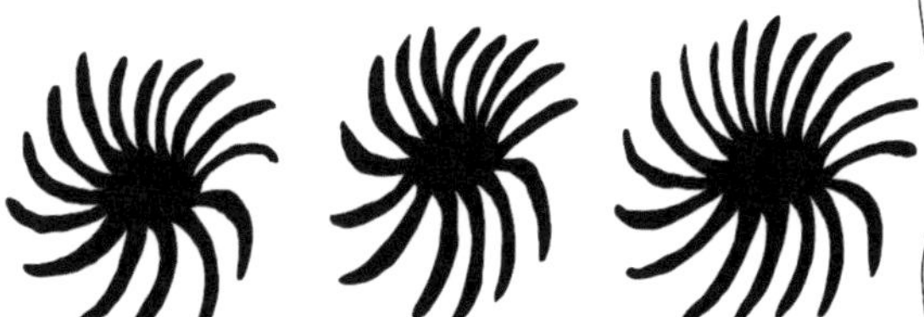

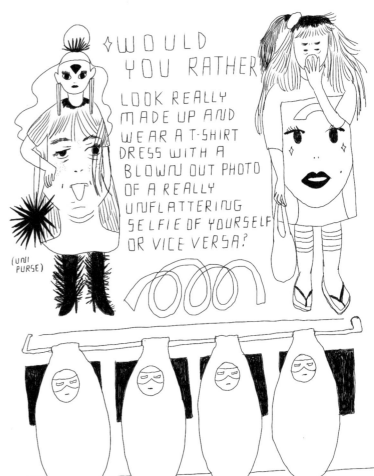

◊ WOULD YOU RATHER LOOK REALLY MADE UP AND WEAR A T-SHIRT DRESS WITH A BLOWN OUT PHOTO OF A REALLY UNFLATTERING SELFIE OF YOURSELF OR VICE VERSA?

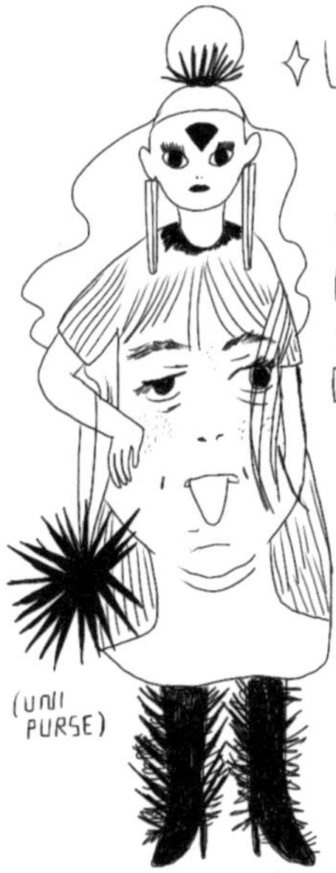
(UNI PURSE)

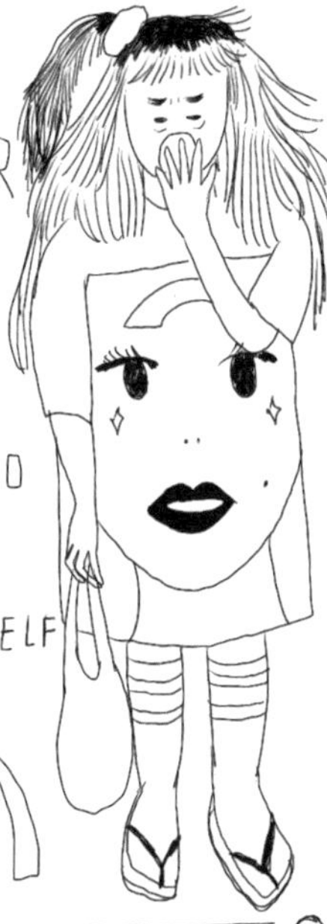

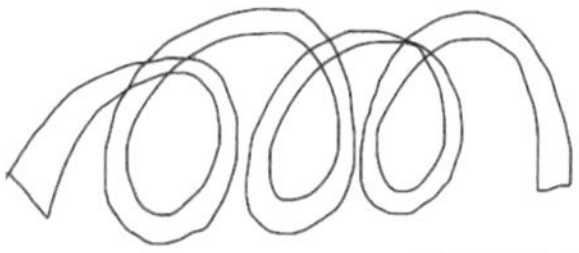

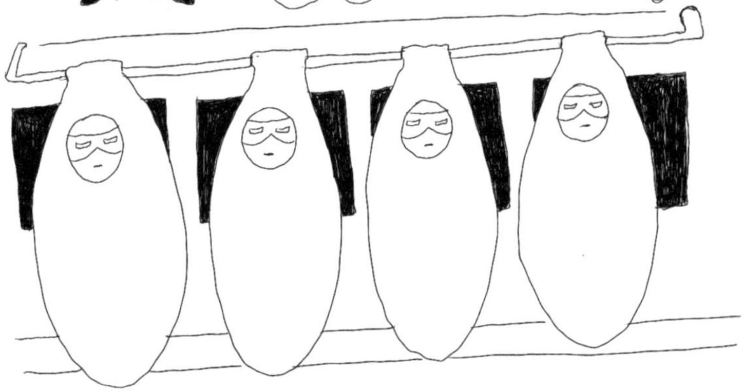

◊ COMMUTER COCCOON SLEEPING POD COAT

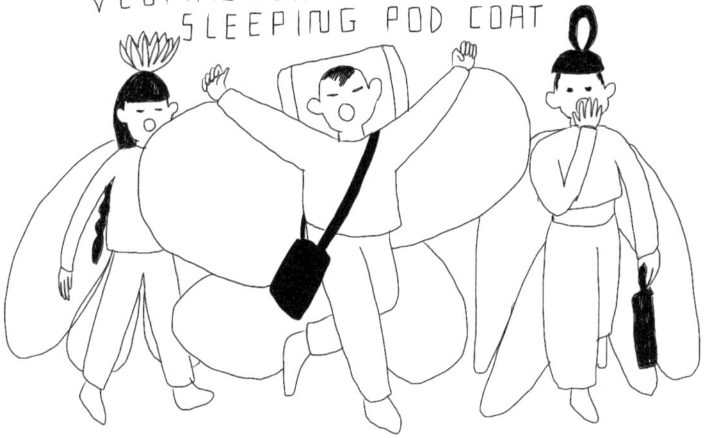

◊ UNFOLDS MAGICALLY TO REVEAL BUTTERFLY WINGS

ENAMEL PINS REPRESENTING VERY SPECIFIC EMOTIONS, EXPERIENCES, THOUGHTS, NEUROSES, INSECURITIES, HOPES, SECRET DREAMS, DESIRES, ETC. A SECRET VISUAL CODE KNOWN ONLY TO A SMALL SUBCULTURE OF LONELY PEOPLE ON A GLOBAL NETWORK

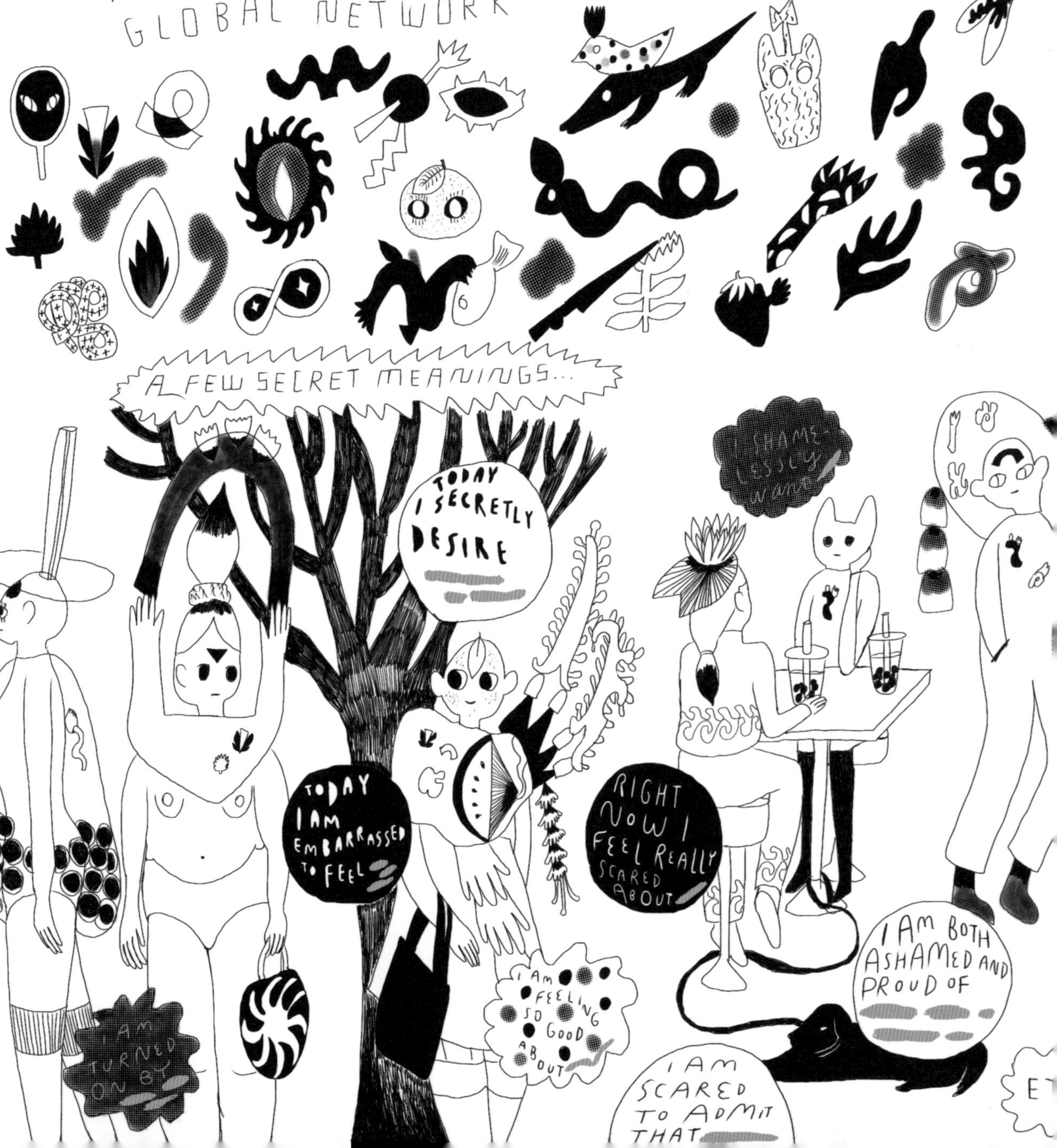
A FEW SECRET MEANINGS...
TODAY I SECRETLY DESIRE
I SHAMELESSLY WANT
TODAY I AM EMBARRASSED TO FEEL
RIGHT NOW I FEEL REALLY SCARED ABOUT
I AM BOTH ASHAMED AND PROUD OF
I AM FEELING SO GOOD ABOUT
I AM TURNED ON BY
I AM SCARED TO ADMIT THAT
ET

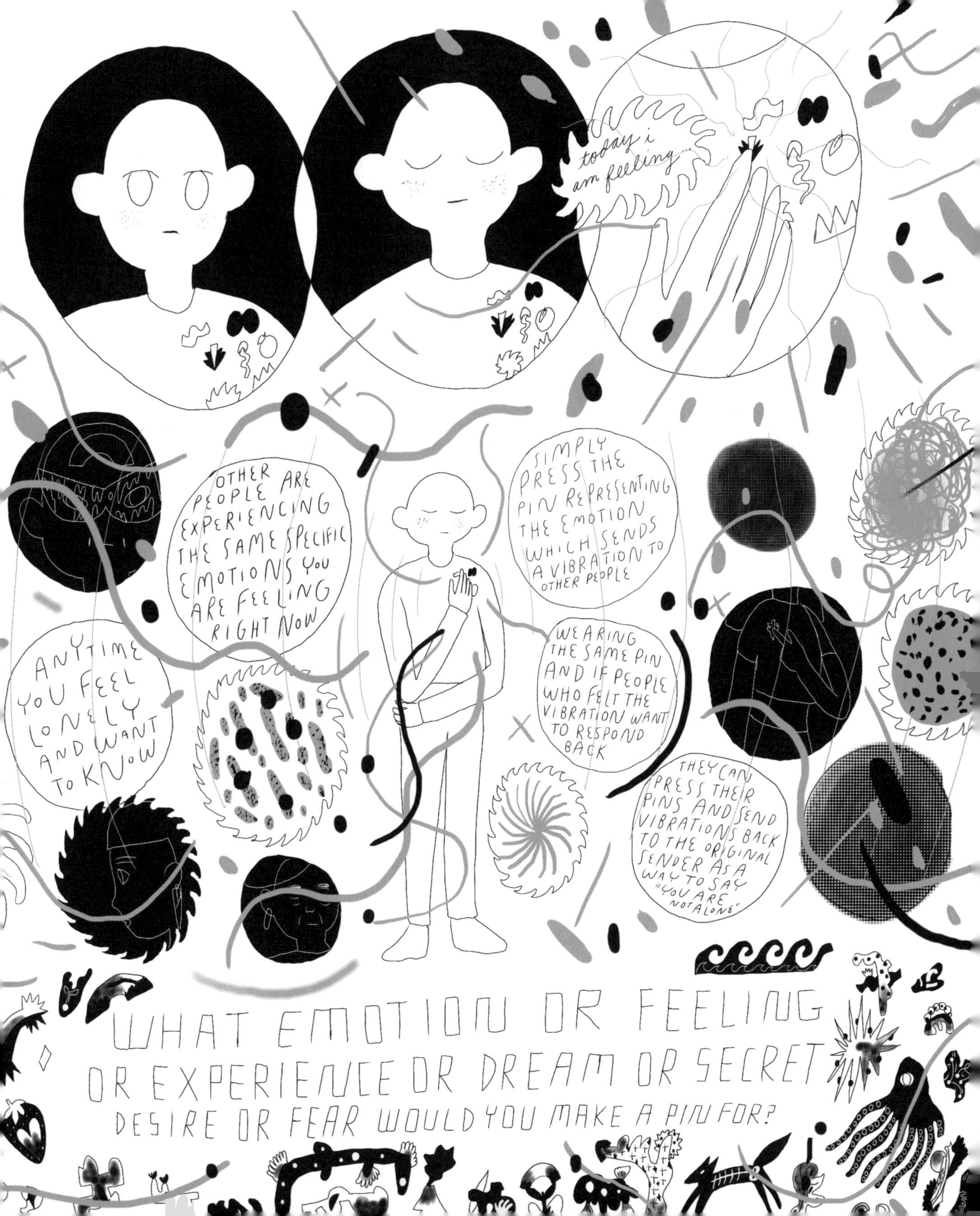
today i am feeling...
ANYTIME YOU FEEL LONELY AND WANT TO KNOW
OTHER PEOPLE ARE EXPERIENCING THE SAME SPECIFIC EMOTIONS YOU ARE FEELING RIGHT NOW
SIMPLY PRESS THE PIN REPRESENTING THE EMOTION WHICH SENDS A VIBRATION TO OTHER PEOPLE
WEARING THE SAME PIN AND IF PEOPLE WHO FELT THE VIBRATION WANT TO RESPOND BACK
THEY CAN PRESS THEIR PINS AND SEND VIBRATIONS BACK TO THE ORIGINAL SENDER AS A WAY TO SAY "YOU ARE NOT ALONE"
WHAT EMOTION OR FEELING OR EXPERIENCE OR DREAM OR SECRET DESIRE OR FEAR WOULD YOU MAKE A PIN FOR?

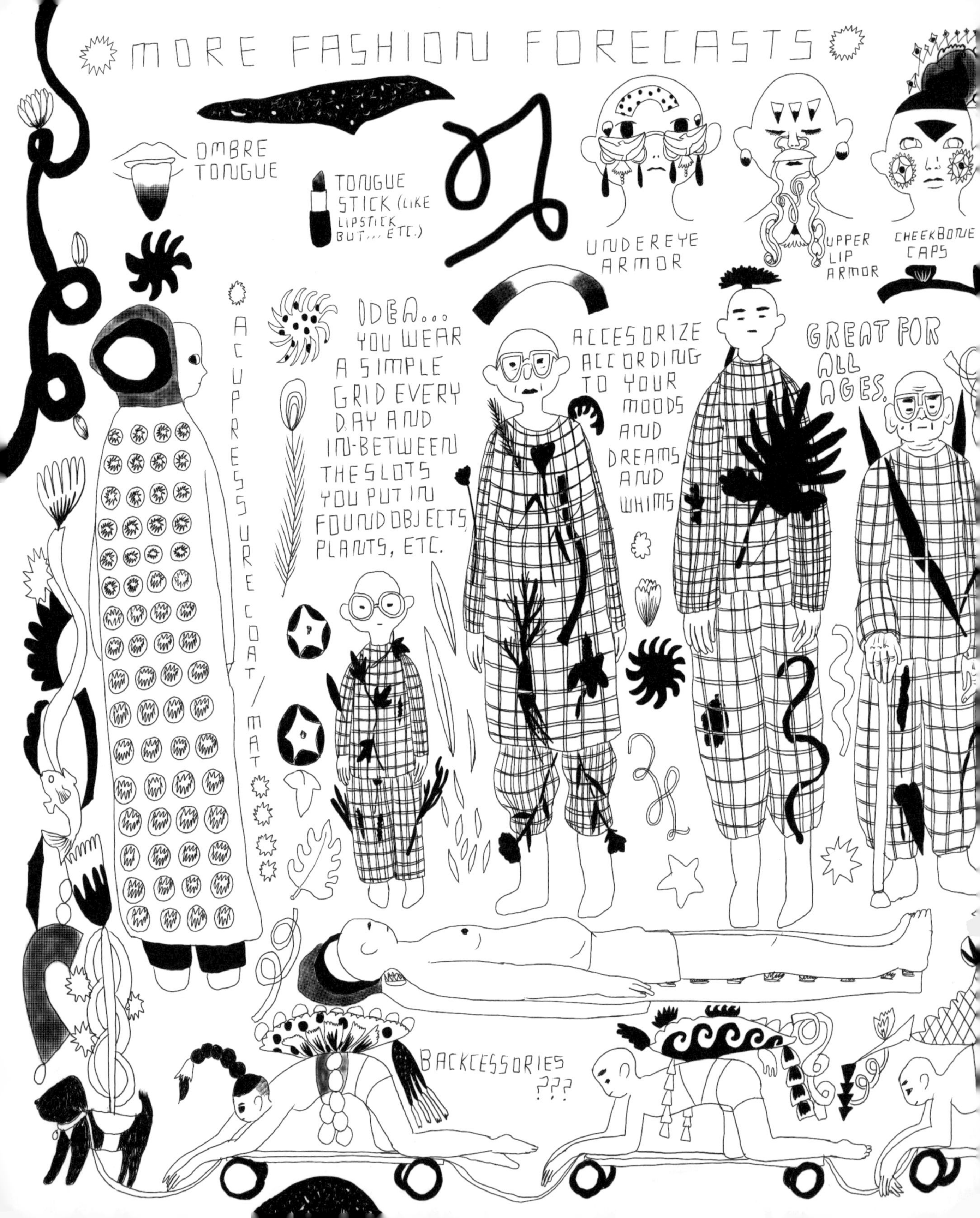
MORE FASHION FORECASTS
OMBRE TONGUE
TONGUE STICK (LIKE LIPSTICK BUT... ETC.)
UNDEREYE ARMOR
UPPER LIP ARMOR
CHEEKBONE CAPS
ACUPRESSURE COAT / MAT
IDEA... YOU WEAR A SIMPLE GRID EVERY DAY AND IN-BETWEEN THE SLOTS YOU PUT IN FOUND OBJECTS, PLANTS, ETC.
ACCESORIZE ACCORDING TO YOUR MOODS AND DREAMS AND WHIMS
GREAT FOR ALL AGES.
BACKCESSORIES ???

MORE FASHION FORECASTS
BODY HAIR EDITION

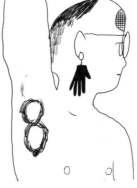

✧ THE "VALENTINE"

✧ THE "I'M A PISCES"

✧ THE "I BELIEVE IN REINCARNATION AND THE AFTERLIFE, ETC."

✳ ARMPIT HAIR PATCHES COLORED AND SHAVED INTO SHAPES TO DEPICT YOUR MOOD, INTERESTS, PERSONALITY, ETC.

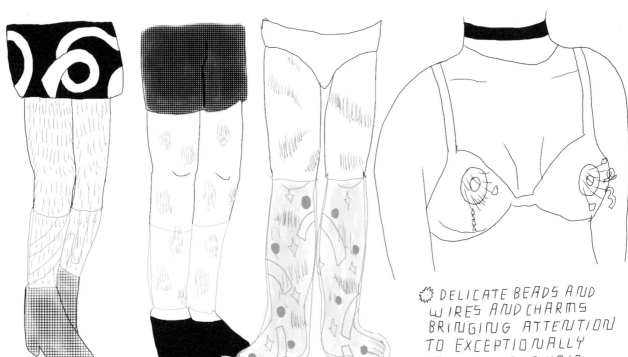

✳ NEON LEG HAIR

✳ NEON LEG HAIR SHAVED INTO PATTERNS

✳ DELICATE BEADS AND WIRES AND CHARMS BRINGING ATTENTION TO EXCEPTIONALLY LONG NIPPLE HAIR

Menstrual Fashion Edition

- RED SPIKY ONESIE FOR PMS DAYS

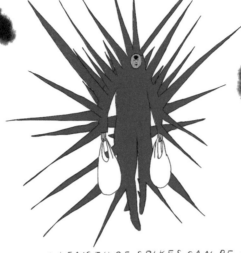

- LENGTH OF SPIKES CAN BE ADJUSTED ACCORDING TO SEVERITY OF SYMPTOMS

- OPTIONAL RESTING DEMON FACE MASK FOR RELIEF FROM POLITE EMOTING & SMALL TALK

- NO SPIKE VERSION FOR ROLLING AROUND IN BED AT HOME. INCLUDES SUPPLY OF EXTRA SOFT TISSUE THAT COMES OUT OF SLIT OPENING FROM THE STOMACH AREA

- DECORATING AND PUBLICLY DISPLAYING YOUR PERIOD STAINS WITH DECALS, RHINESTONES, AND FLOWERS

- EMERGENCY MENSTRUAL CUP/ TAMPON EARRING AND NECKLACE SET

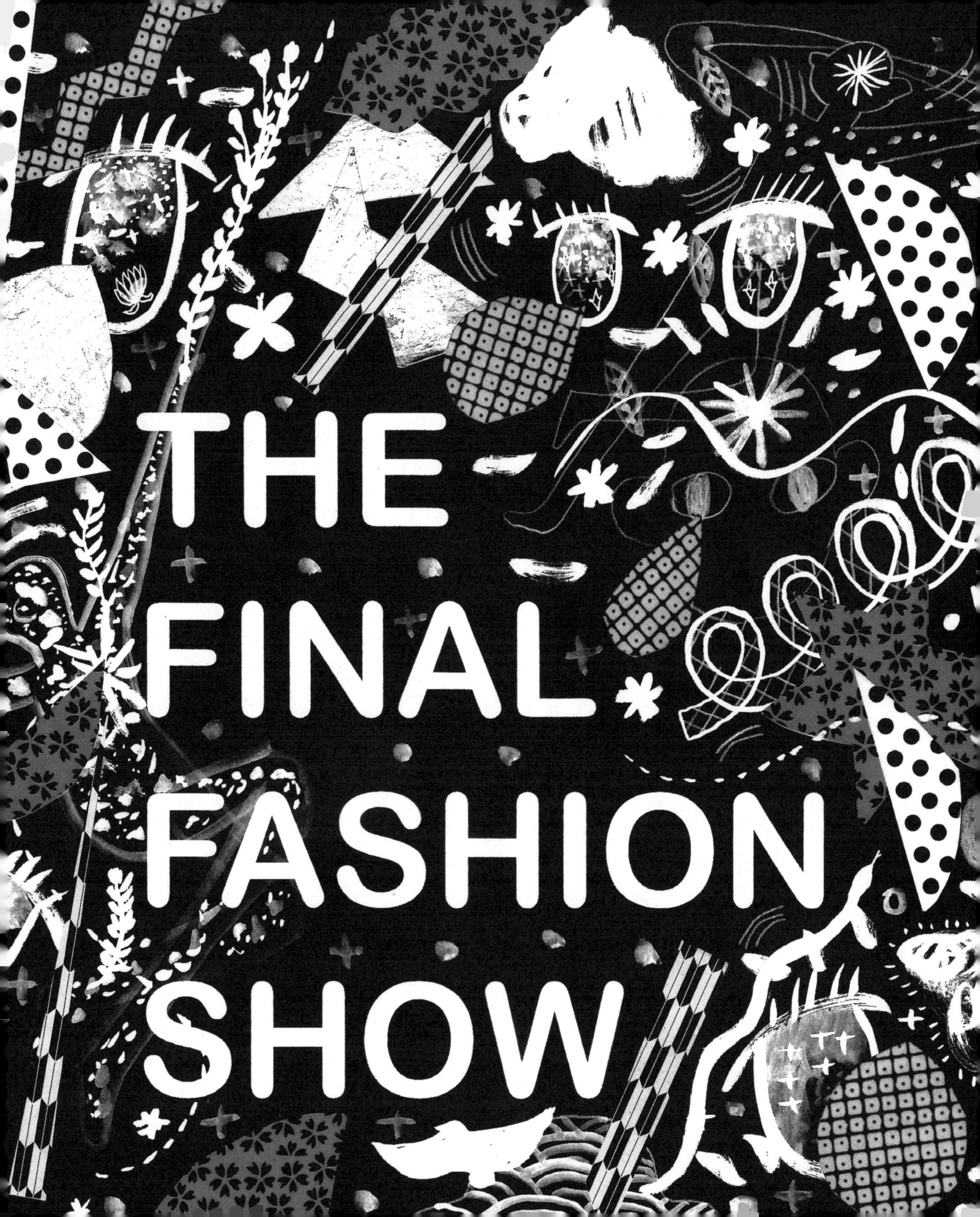
THE
FINAL
FASHION
SHOW

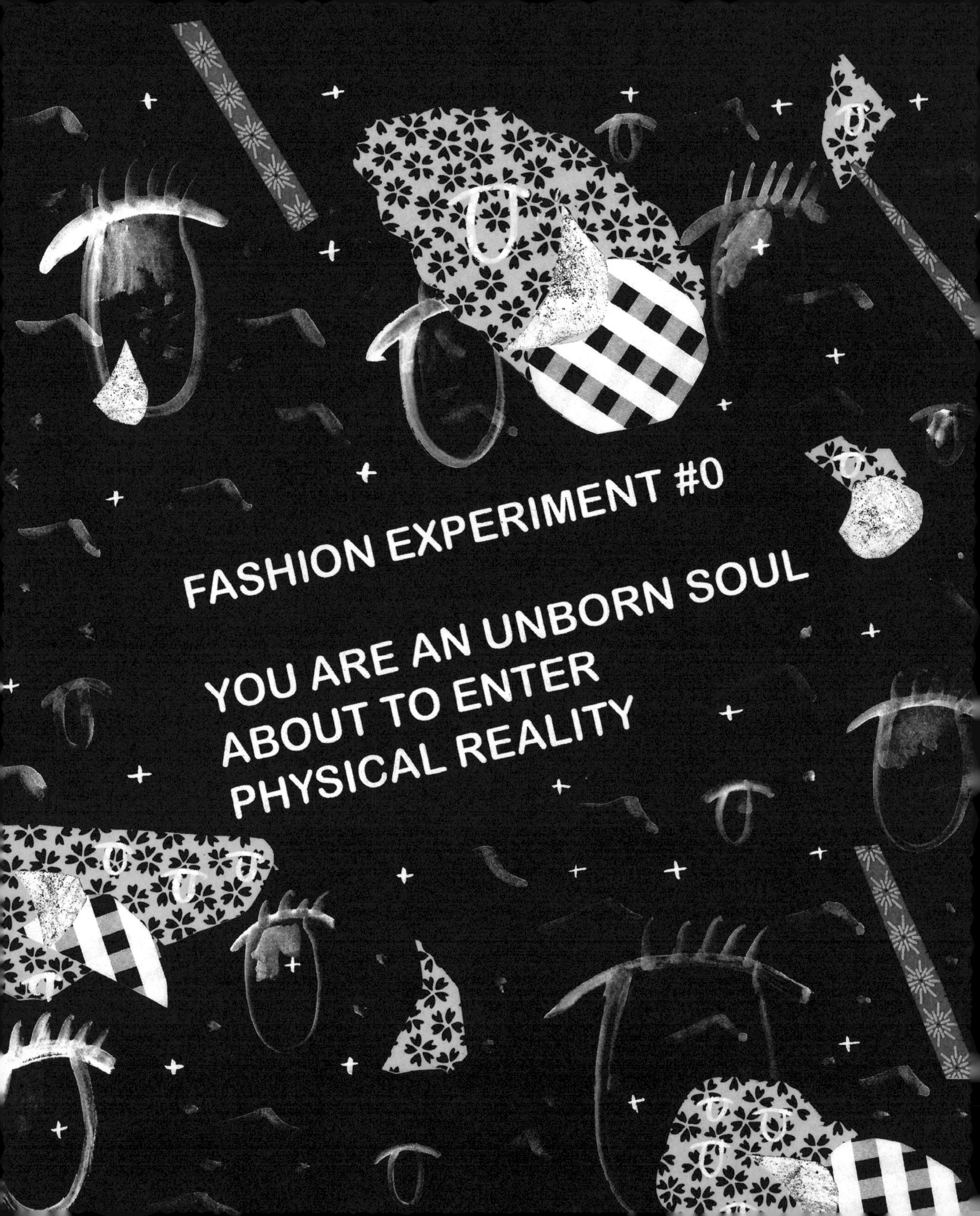
FASHION EXPERIMENT #0
YOU ARE AN UNBORN SOUL
ABOUT TO ENTER
PHYSICAL REALITY

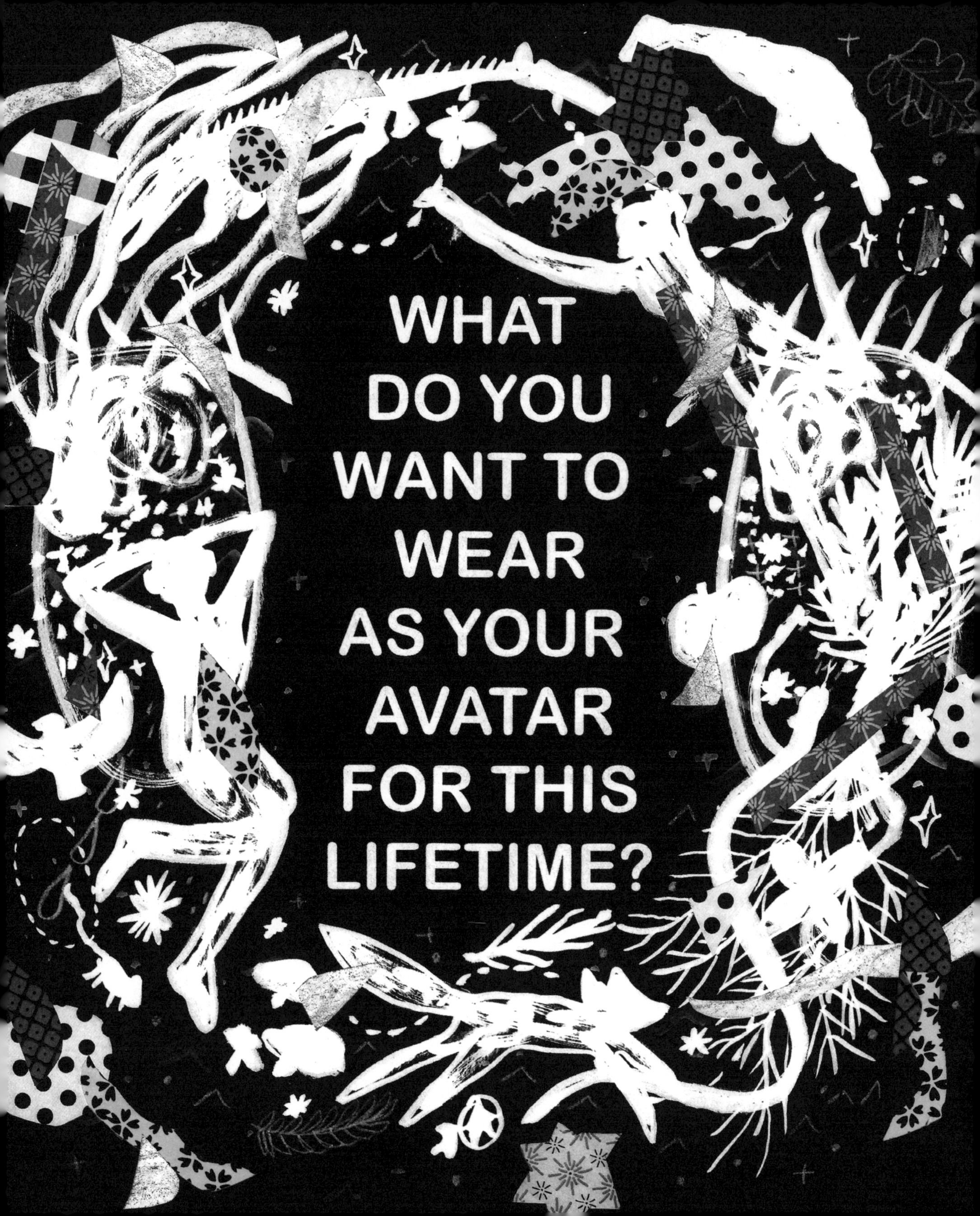
WHAT
DO YOU
WANT TO
WEAR
AS YOUR
AVATAR
FOR THIS
LIFETIME?

IF YOU ARE NOT HAPPY WITH YOUR AVATAR, DON'T WORRY.

IDENTITES ARE ALWAYS IN FLUX.

EVERYTHING ALWAYS CHANGES.

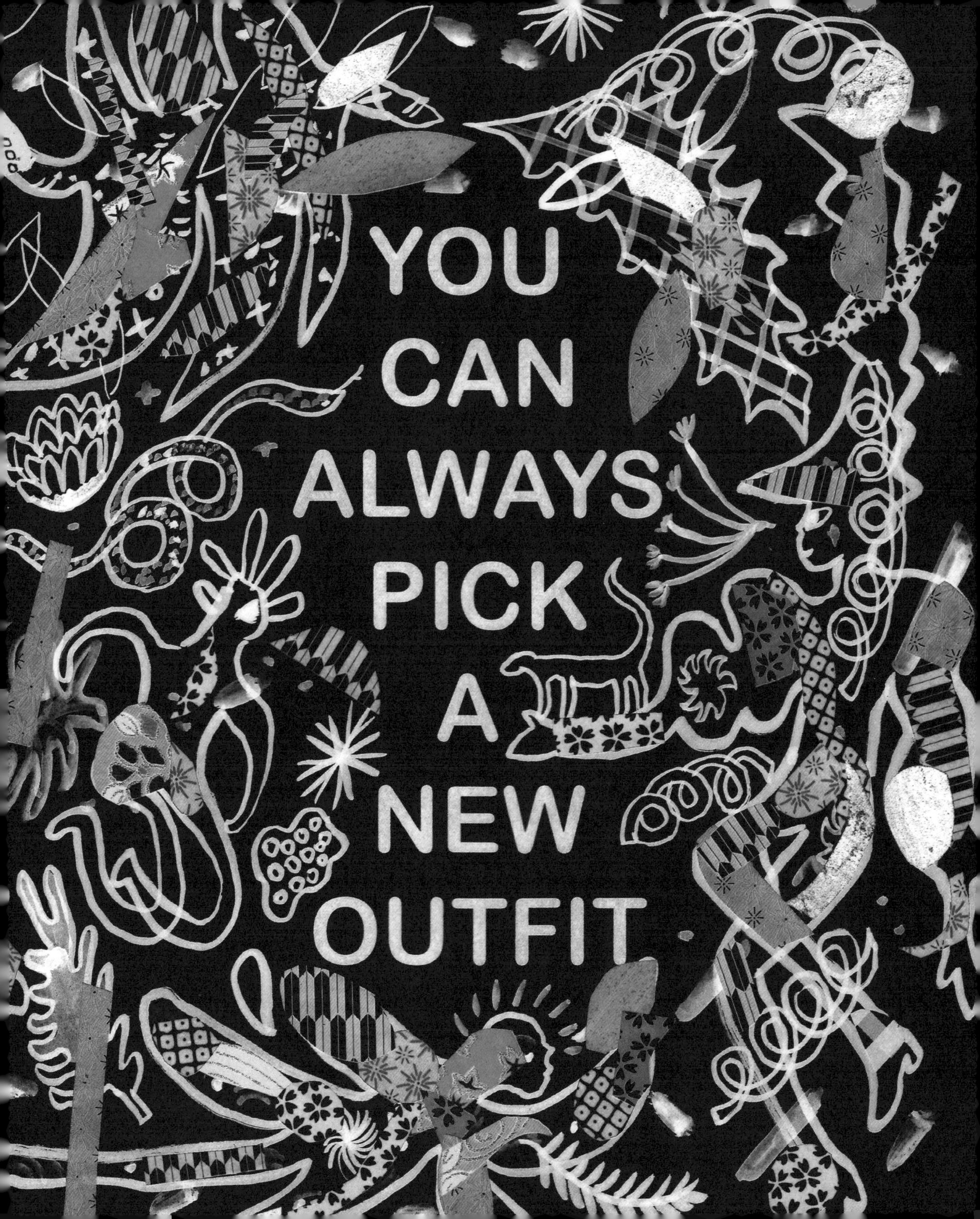
YOU CAN ALWAYS PICK A NEW OUTFIT

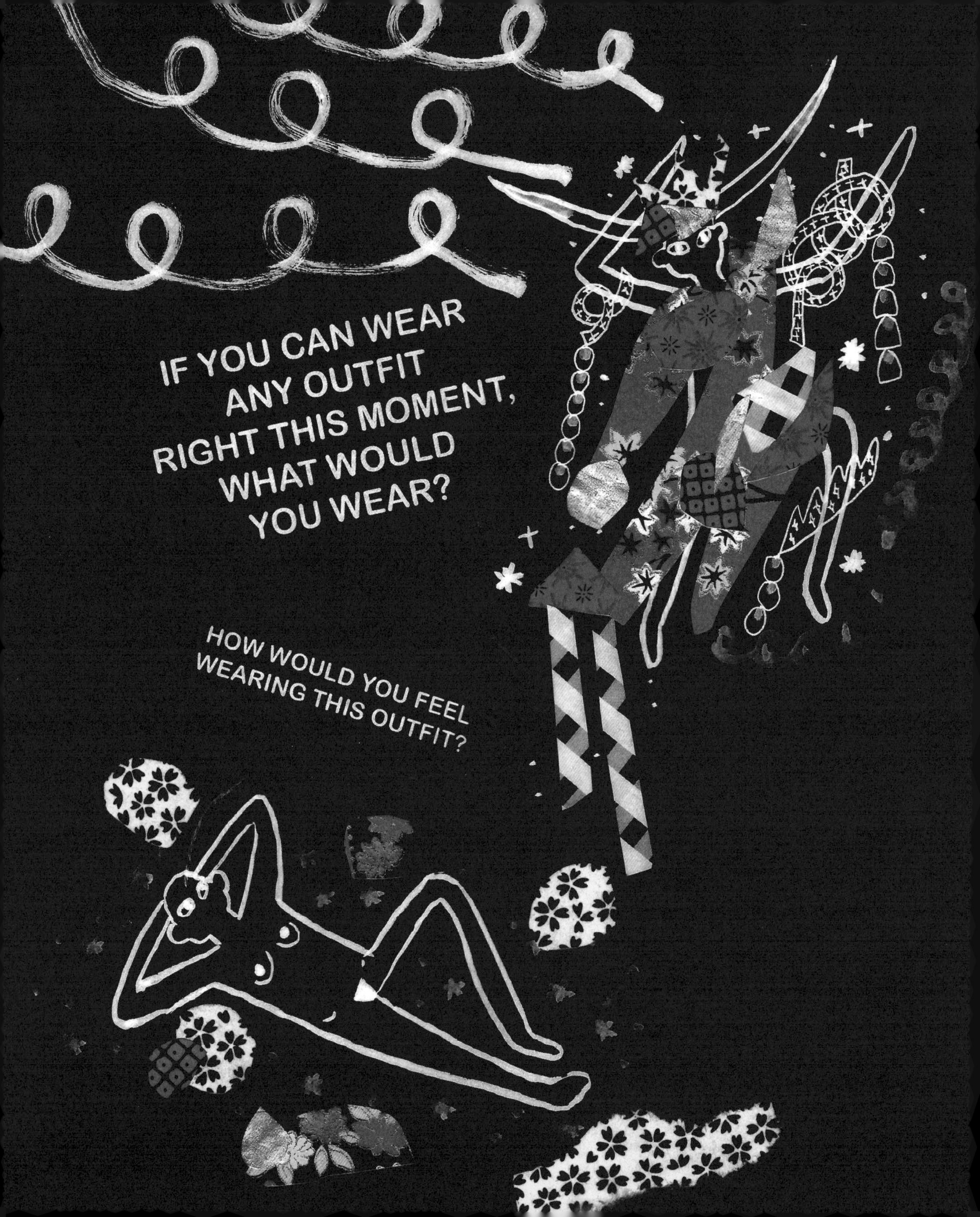
IF YOU CAN WEAR
ANY OUTFIT
RIGHT THIS MOMENT,
WHAT WOULD
YOU WEAR?
HOW WOULD YOU FEEL
WEARING THIS OUTFIT?

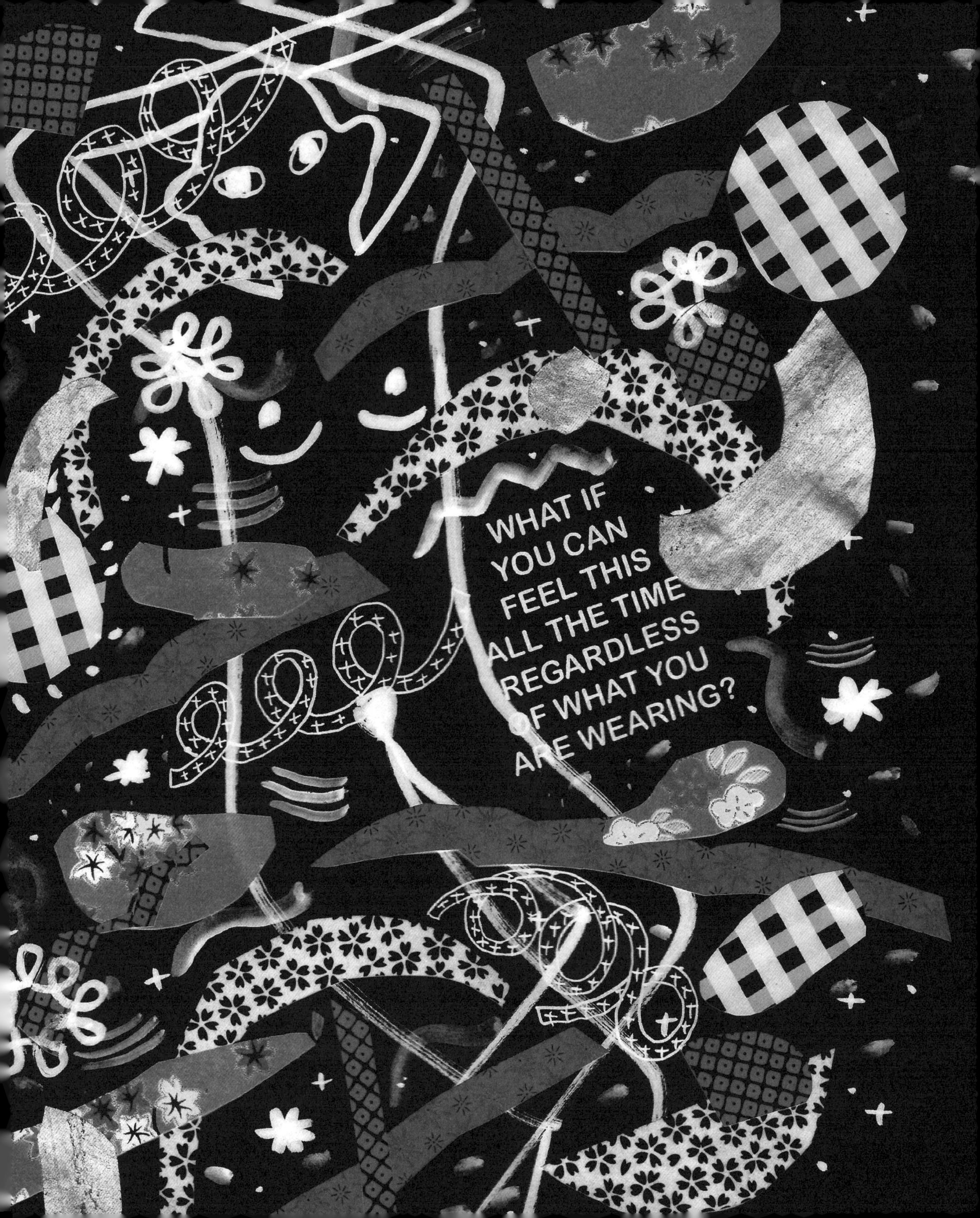
WHAT IF
YOU CAN
FEEL THIS
ALL THE TIME
REGARDLESS
OF WHAT YOU
ARE WEARING?

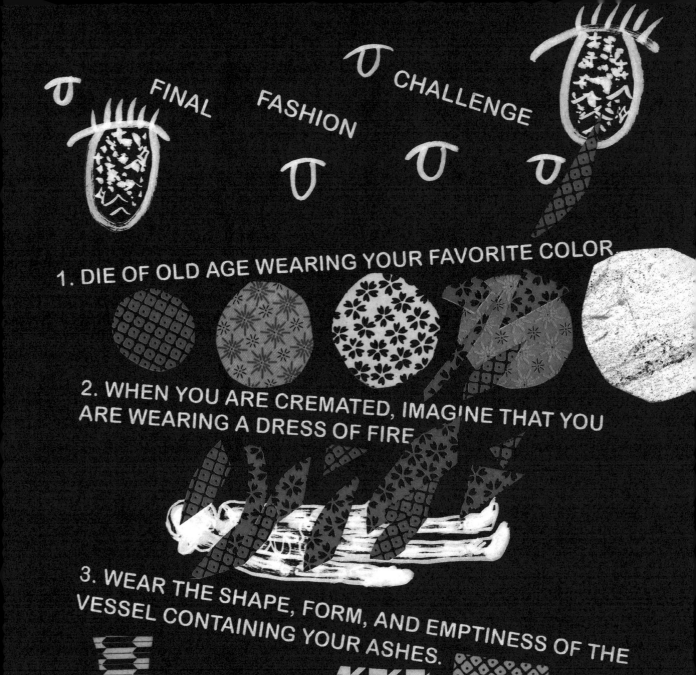

FINAL FASHION CHALLENGE

1. DIE OF OLD AGE WEARING YOUR FAVORITE COLOR

2. WHEN YOU ARE CREMATED, IMAGINE THAT YOU ARE WEARING A DRESS OF FIRE

3. WEAR THE SHAPE, FORM, AND EMPTINESS OF THE VESSEL CONTAINING YOUR ASHES.

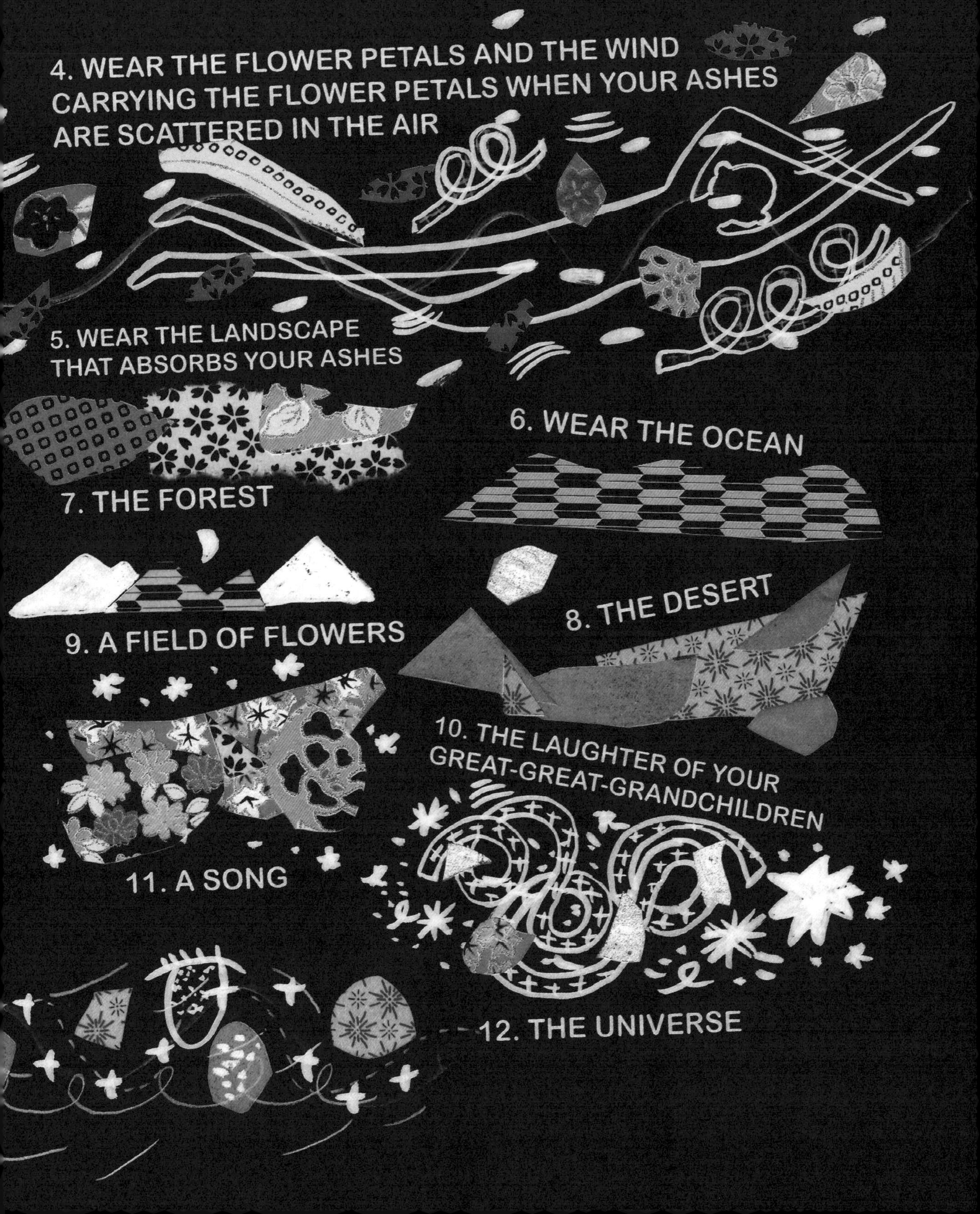
4. WEAR THE FLOWER PETALS AND THE WIND CARRYING THE FLOWER PETALS WHEN YOUR ASHES ARE SCATTERED IN THE AIR
5. WEAR THE LANDSCAPE THAT ABSORBS YOUR ASHES
6. WEAR THE OCEAN
7. THE FOREST
8. THE DESERT
9. A FIELD OF FLOWERS
10. THE LAUGHTER OF YOUR GREAT-GREAT-GRANDCHILDREN
11. A SONG
12. THE UNIVERSE

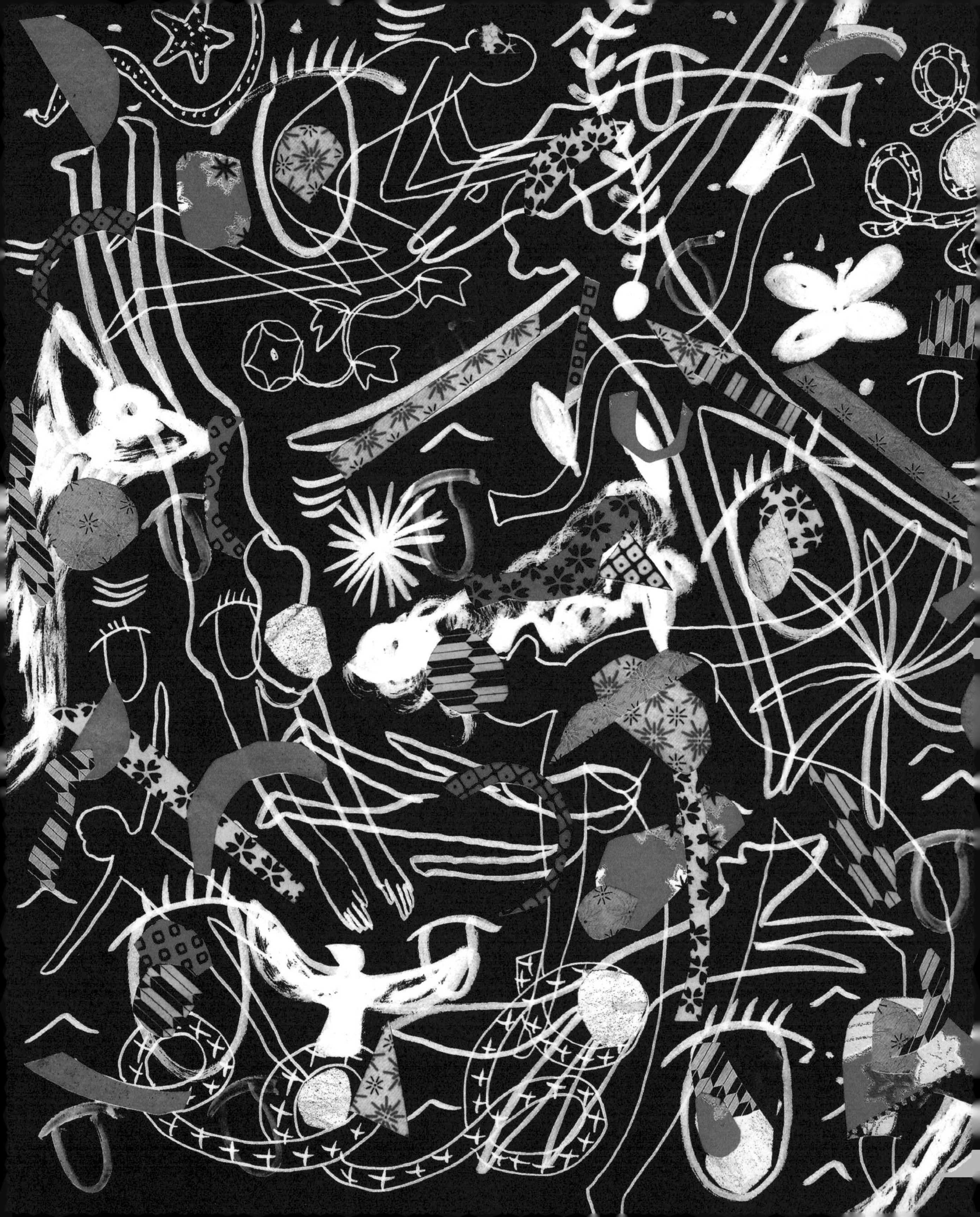

ACKNOWLEDGMENTS

THANK YOU TO THE FOLLOWING INDIVIDUALS AND ORGANIZATIONS AND ENTITIES

ADRIEL LUIS AND THE SMITHSONIAN ASIAN
PACIFIC AMERICAN CENTER

ROBBIE MONSOD

DAVID CHIEN

JARED SMITH

BASECAMP DC

FAMILY, ANCESTORS, SPIRIT GUIDES, EARTH

+ + +

PHOTOGRAPHS ON PAGES 40-41, 46 BY LES TALUSAN

ALL CLOTHING AND PROPS IN INSTALLATION HANDCRAFTED BY ROBBIE MONSOD IN LOS ANGELES

VIDEO EDITING IN INSTALLATION BY DAVID CHIEN

"AM I BEING A 'FASHION QUESTION' OR A 'FASHION STATEMENT'?" COURTESY OF KRISTA SUH

FASHION FORECAST WAS ORIGINALLY COMMISSIONED AS A ZINE AND INSTALLATION FOR
CROSSLINES: A CULTURE LAB ON INTERSECTIONALITY, PRESENTED BY
THE SMITHSONIAN ASIAN PACIFIC AMERICAN CENTER IN MAY 2016 AT THE SMITHSONIAN
ARTS & INDUSTRIES BUILDING

YUMI SAKUGAWA
IS AN ARTIST
LIVING IN LOS ANGELES

@YUMISAKUGAWA
YUMISAKUGAWA.COM